M000208030

# BLESSINGS
## — *for the* —
# MORNING & EVENING

*Life-Giving Words of Encouragement*
*to Begin and End Your Day*

# SUSIE LARSON

BETHANY HOUSE PUBLISHERS
*a division of Baker Publishing Group*
Minneapolis, Minnesota

Published by Bethany House Publishers
11400 Hampshire Avenue South
Bloomington, Minnesota 55438
www.bethanyhouse.com

Bethany House Publishers is a division of
Baker Publishing Group, Grand Rapids, Michigan

Printed in China

Library of Congress Cataloging-in-Publication Data is on file at the Library of Congress,
Washington, DC.

ISBN: 978-0-7642-3018-9

The material in this book was originally published in *Blessings for the Evening* (2013) and
*Blessings for the Morning* (2014) by Susie Larson.

Cover photography by Amy Weiss/Arcangel; other images © Shutterstock Photography
Cover design and interior art direction by Paul Higdon

Author is represented by The Steve Laube Agency

17  18  19  20  21  22  23      7  6  5  4  3  2  1

To my beautiful and beloved sons—
Jake, Luke, and Jordan.
Love you so, and always will.


To Jesus
May You breathe fresh life into every soul
who picks up this book.
Knowing that we get to spend eternity
with You is the greatest blessing of all.
You're our greatest treasure.

# Contents

## Blessings for the Evening

## Blessings for Specific Needs and Occasions

# *To You, My Friend*

God loves you with an everlasting love. He is
faithful, wise, and true. He is a miracle-working,
soul-saving, life-transforming God. And He
cares deeply about you.

As you work your way through these pages,
may you grow to know—on a much deeper
level—what you possess when you have Christ.
He is above all, in all, and through all. He is
the way, the truth, and the life. He promises
never to leave you, never to forsake you, and
never to let go of your hand. Life on earth is
hard sometimes, but life with God is always
good, always beautiful, and forever eternal.
The Lord wants you to last long and finish
strong, and He's the one who will keep you
strong to the end.

May these blessings be yours in every way.

—*Susie Larson*

# Blessings for the Morning
## and Evening

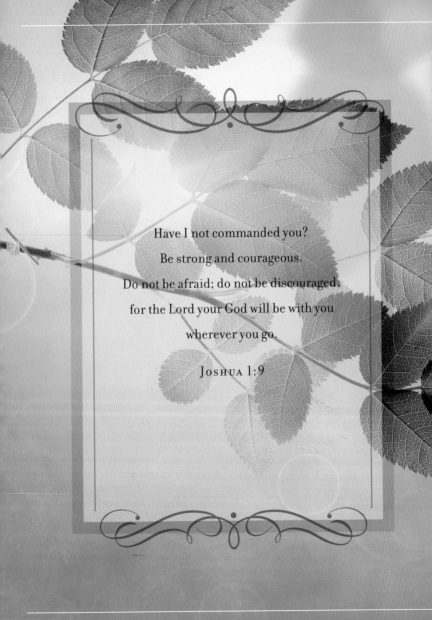

Have I not commanded you?

Be strong and courageous.

Do not be afraid; do not be discouraged,

for the Lord your God will be with you

wherever you go.

JOSHUA 1:9

# Persevere With Feisty Faith

May you make up your mind to persevere and not quit.

May you refuse to be bullied by your fears or diminished by your insecurities.

May you rise up in the knowledge that God made a masterpiece when He made you!

May you embrace the grace to abound in every good work in spite of enemy opposition.

Overwhelming victory belongs to you because you belong to Him.

Walk with feisty faith today! He's got you.

I am convinced that nothing can ever
separate us from God's love. Neither
death nor life, neither angels nor
demons, neither our fears for today nor
our worries about tomorrow—not even
the powers of hell can separate us from
God's love. No power in the sky above or
in the earth below—indeed, nothing in
all creation will ever be able to separate
us from the love of God that is revealed
in Christ Jesus our Lord.

ROMANS 8:38–39 NLT

## God's Unshakable Love

May the Lord awaken you to fresh and powerful
revelations of His love.

May He stir in you a deep desire to read His Word
and stand on His promises.

May He lift you up so you can see your life from His
perspective.

May He put a joy in your heart that makes you glad
and others smile.

And tonight, may you wrap yourself up in this wonderful truth: Absolutely nothing can separate you
from His love!

Sleep well.

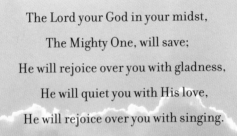

The Lord your God in your midst,

The Mighty One, will save;

He will rejoice over you with gladness,

He will quiet you with His love,

He will rejoice over you with singing.

Zephaniah 3:17 NKJV

# Heaven Rejoices Over You

May you—in spite of your critics—move forward in faith.

May God's song over your life drown out every lesser voice.

May you look up and rejoice because heaven rejoices over you.
Remember who you are today!

In Christ Jesus you possess all you need.

Your name is written on His hand.

Your desires are especially close to His heart.

His call on your life fits you perfectly.

Be watchful and thankful today.

Jesus is with you.

There is no condemnation for those who belong to Christ Jesus. And because you belong to him, the power of the life-giving Spirit has freed you from the power of sin that leads to death. . . . The Spirit of God, who raised Jesus from the dead, lives in you. And just as God raised Christ Jesus from the dead, he will give life to your mortal bodies by this same Spirit living within you.

ROMANS 8:1–2, 11 NLT

# A Brand-New You

May God's opinion matter far more to you than man's opinion.

May His dreams for you speak louder than your fears.

May His forgiveness wash over every sin from your past.

And may you rise up in the morning with the knowledge that He's made you brand-new, through and through.

No spot or stain on you!

Rest well tonight.

And Jabez called on the God of Israel saying, "Oh, that You would bless me indeed, and enlarge my territory, that Your hand would be with me, and that You would keep me from evil, that I may not cause pain!" So God granted him what he requested.

1 Chronicles 4:10 NKJV

## Blessed in Every Way

May the Lord enlarge your territory, expand your influence,
and increase your capacity to walk in faith.

May His hand of power be upon you in a way that marks
everything you do.

May He keep you from harm—both causing and
enduring it—and may He use you to bless a world very
much in need.

May He surprise you with breakthroughs and
still-water Sabbath moments.

Your Shepherd has placed His hand of blessing
upon your head, and He will faithfully lead you.

Have a lighthearted, joy-filled day today!

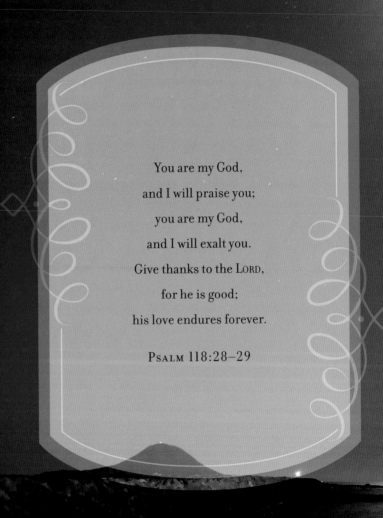

You are my God,

and I will praise you;

you are my God,

and I will exalt you.

Give thanks to the LORD,

for he is good;

his love endures forever.

PSALM 118:28–29

# The Lord's Goodness

May the Lord bless you with deep, nourishing sleep tonight.

May you wake up fresh and renewed, ready to face the day.

May you find the time to pause in His presence, listen for His voice, and give Him thanks for all He's done and for all He's about to do.

You are His beloved, and He is yours.

His banner over you is love!

Sleep well tonight.

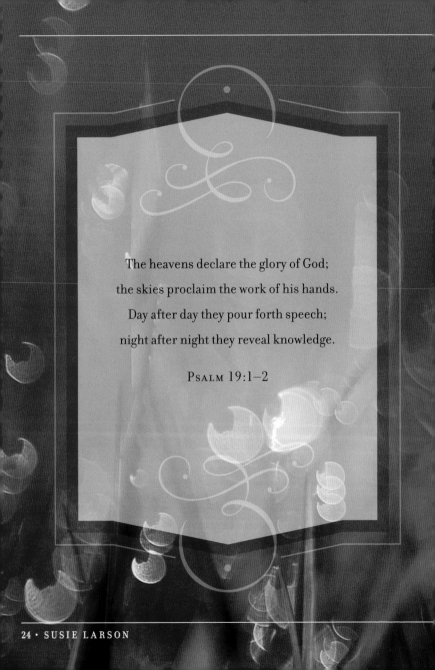

The heavens declare the glory of God;

the skies proclaim the work of his hands.

Day after day they pour forth speech;

night after night they reveal knowledge.

PSALM 19:1–2

# Ready for a Change

As the winds of change start to blow in your life, may you lean in and listen for the voice of the Lord.

Instead of looking for "signs" and mistakenly drawing the wrong conclusion, may you instead look to the Lord and His strength.

He'll speak to you in a way you'll understand.

God will lead you in the way you should go. He is faithful and true, and He's doing a NEW thing in your life!

Keep an ear bent toward heaven. Daily the heavens pour forth speech. May you listen for every word.

Blessings on your day today!

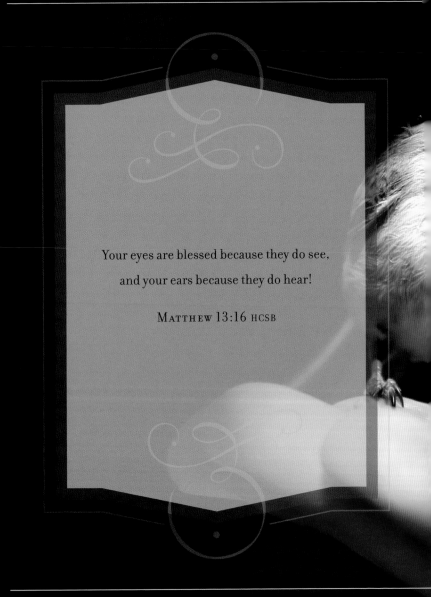

Your eyes are blessed because they do see,

and your ears because they do hear!

MATTHEW 13:16 HCSB

# Seeing and Hearing God

May God bless your eyes so you begin to see
everyone and everything redemptively.

May God bless your ears so you'll only
hear words consistent with His voice and
His song over your life.

May God bless your heart that you may be
a wellspring of life for others.

And may God bless your hands and feet
that you may tend to His business during
your time on earth.

Your life matters deeply to Him.

Rest in that fact.

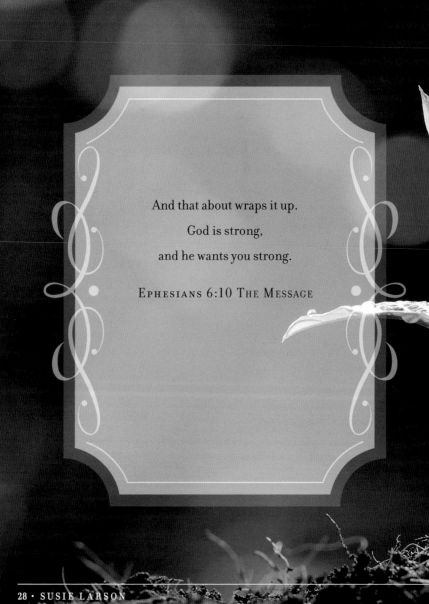

And that about wraps it up.

God is strong,

and he wants you strong.

EPHESIANS 6:10 THE MESSAGE

# He Wants You Strong

May you remember today—above everything else—that the One who put the stars in place greatly delights in you. He is strong and powerful and gentle and true.

Today, may you refuse to wonder if He cares, because He truly, truly does.

May you soak in the reality of His presence and His love today.

May you read books, listen to music, and enjoy the company of those who remind you who you are in Him; it'll strengthen your soul!

And may you steward this day in a way that replenishes you for the journey ahead.

Have a great day.

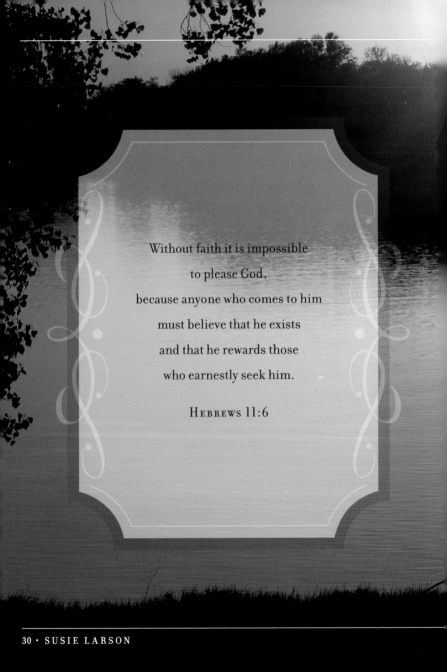

Without faith it is impossible
to please God,
because anyone who comes to him
must believe that he exists
and that he rewards those
who earnestly seek him.

HEBREWS 11:6

# Heaven Is on Your Side

May you learn to trust God in increasing measures.

When He calls, may you follow where He leads, step out without having all of the information, speak up without having all the answers, and look up when your circumstances threaten to weigh you down.

May you live, breathe, and speak as one who is ensured victory and equipped to do the impossible.

Sleep well tonight, knowing that all of heaven is on your side.

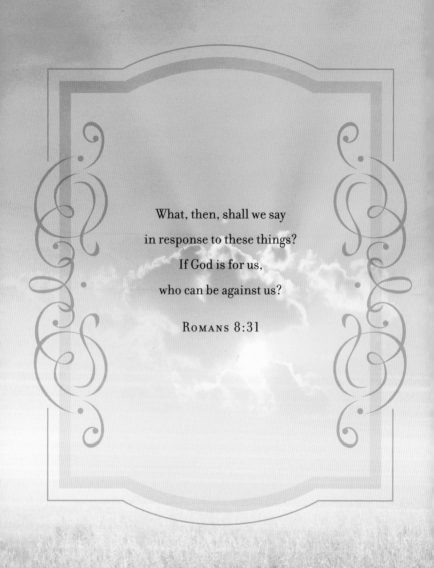

What, then, shall we say
in response to these things?
If God is for us,
who can be against us?

ROMANS 8:31

# Look Up and Sing

When you are tempted to look down in despair, may you instead look up and declare, "My God is for me, who can stand against me?"

When you are tempted to whine and grumble, may you instead dance and sing.

When you are tempted to gossip or be petty, may you instead pray and intercede.

God wants to bless the world through you!

Look up today and rejoice. All of heaven is on your side.

Come to Me, all of you

who are weary and burdened,

and I will give you rest.

Matthew 11:28 HCSB

# A Healthy Rhythm

May the Lord establish in you a healthy, divine rhythm of life.

May He strengthen you in mind, body, and spirit.

Where you're broken, may He restore; where you're weary, may He refresh; where you're fearful, may He revive faith.

May your coming days be far more blessed than your former days.

Sleep well tonight. There will be new mercies waiting for you in the morning.

Praise the Lord, my soul; all
my inmost being, praise his holy
name. Praise the Lord, my soul, and
forget not all his benefits—who forgives all
your sins and heals all your diseases, who redeems your life from the pit and crowns you
with love and compassion, who satisfies your
desires with good things so that your youth is
renewed like the eagle's.

PSALM 103:1–5

# His Grace Strengthens You

May the Lord's grace and power make you bold and courageous.

May He remove from your midst sickness, despair, and disorder of every kind.

May He bring clarity, peace, and joy to your heart and mind.

And may your faith bring pleasure to His heart.

Have a great day!

Remember this:

Whoever sows sparingly

will also reap sparingly,

and whoever sows generously

will also reap generously.

Each of you should give what you

have decided in your heart to give,

not reluctantly or under compulsion,

for God loves a cheerful giver.

2 Corinthians 9:6–7

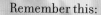

## Sowing and Reaping

May God give you faith to sow seeds.

May you become a purposeful, generous, faith-filled sower.

May
He supply and in-
crease your store of seed
and enlarge the harvest of your
righteousness.

May you be made rich in every way, generous in every occasion, and leave the world thanking God for your faithful soul!

Rest well tonight, knowing your Father in heaven possesses all.

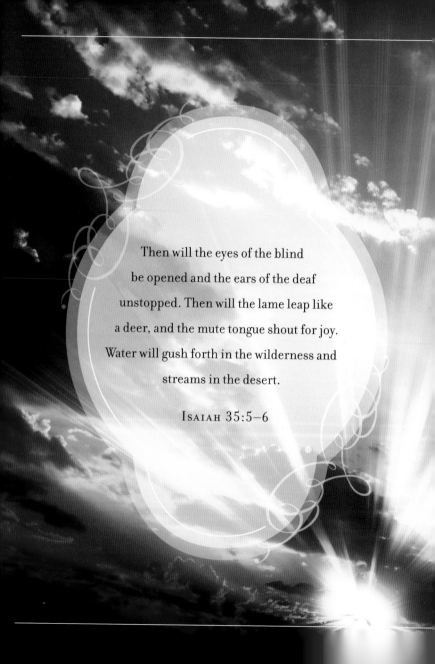

Then will the eyes of the blind
be opened and the ears of the deaf
unstopped. Then will the lame leap like
a deer, and the mute tongue shout for joy.
Water will gush forth in the wilderness and
streams in the desert.

ISAIAH 35:5–6

# *Believe for Greater Things*

May you truly believe that God is up to something good in your life.

May the impossible suddenly seem possible.

May you envision the lost being found, the sick made well, and the poor made truly rich in Christ Jesus.

You are the object of God's great affection and provision.

You matter to Him more than you can comprehend.

Have a joy-filled day today.

Since we are surrounded by such a huge crowd of witnesses to the life of faith, let us strip off every weight that slows us down, especially the sin that so easily trips us up. And let us run with endurance the race God has set before us.

HEBREWS 12:1 NLT

# Stepping Out

May God inspire you to achieve a
goal that He puts in your heart.

May He stir up faith as you
step up and step out.

May He give you fresh conviction and discipline to
say no to lesser things so
you can say yes to His best
plan for you.

May the wind of the Holy
Spirit fill your sail and take
you to a new, inspired place.

And tonight, sleep well.

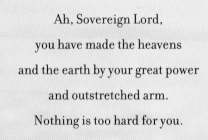

Ah, Sovereign Lord,

you have made the heavens

and the earth by your great power

and outstretched arm.

Nothing is too hard for you.

JEREMIAH 32:17

## God-Moments Everywhere

May salvation spring up all
around you!

May you see lives changed,
relationships restored, and bodies
healed everywhere you turn.

May your expectancy of what God can
and wants to do in your midst rise
exponentially.

He is a star-breathing, miracle-working,
intimately involved God.

Bless your day today.

May you experience the love of Christ,
though it is too great to understand fully.
Then you will be made complete
with all the fullness of life and power
that comes from God.

EPHESIANS 3:19 NLT

# Fresh Joy, Fresh Faith

May the God who created you fill you till you spill
over with fresh joy and perspective.

May the wisdom He imparts to you bless many as
you speak life to those around you.

May He stir up fresh, fiery faith to take on the
mountains and put them under your feet.

Overwhelming victory is yours because *you*
are *His*.

Sleep deeply tonight.

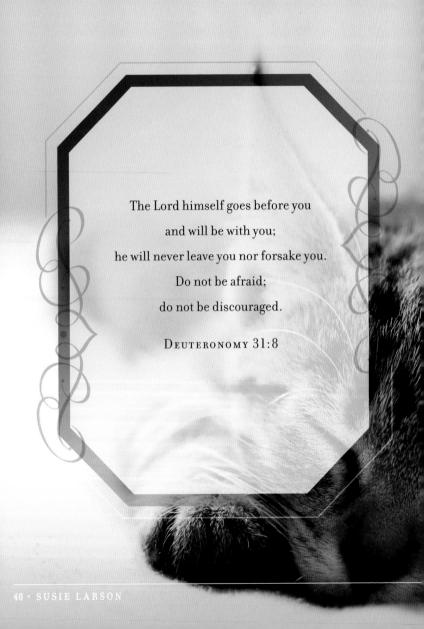

The Lord himself goes before you

and will be with you;

he will never leave you nor forsake you.

Do not be afraid;

do not be discouraged.

DEUTERONOMY 31:8

# Trust Him, He's Got You

May you rise up today with the full assurance that
God has your back.

He is with you, for you, and actively working on your behalf.

He does for you what you cannot do for yourself.

May you do for Him the one thing you can do: Trust Him with
your whole heart and embrace joy along the way.

Grace and peace to you this day!

Praise the Lord, my soul; all my inmost being, praise his holy name. Praise the Lord, my soul, and forget not all his benefits—who forgives all your sins and heals all your diseases, who redeems your life from the pit and crowns you with love and compassion, who satisfies your desires with good things so that your youth is renewed like the eagle's.

Psalm 103:1–5

## A Renewed Life

May the Lord dig up the stones of pain, regret, and angst from your soil and deliver you once and for all.

May He turn over the soil of your heart and plant new seeds of faith, vision, and purpose specific to your life's calling.

May He heal those deep places that nag you.

May He strengthen those weak places that leave you feeling vulnerable.

And may He overwhelm you with a fresh revelation of His love so you can believe that *nothing* is impossible with God on your side!

Sleep well tonight.

Not that I have already obtained all this, or have already arrived at my goal, but I press on to take hold of that for which Christ Jesus took hold of me. Brothers and sisters, I do not consider myself yet to have taken hold of it. But one thing I do: Forgetting what is behind and straining toward what is ahead, I press on toward the goal to win the prize for which God has called me heavenward in Christ Jesus.

PHILIPPIANS 3:12–14

# Embrace Today's Grace

May you refuse to drag the heavy baggage from your past another step.

May you refuse to borrow tomorrow's trouble when it's not yours to carry.

May you instead grab hold of today's mercy, today's grace, and today's power offered you right here, right now, for this moment.

May you walk in the delegated influence God has assigned you.

Walk in a manner worthy of His name.

And may holy confidence and humble dependence mark your life in every way today!

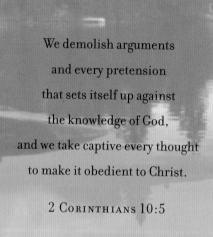

We demolish arguments
and every pretension
that sets itself up against
the knowledge of God,
and we take captive every thought
to make it obedient to Christ.

2 Corinthians 10:5

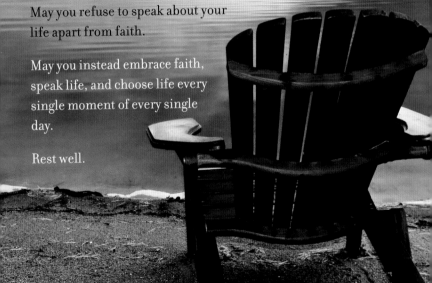

# *Christ in Focus*

May God help you renew your mind and redeem your words.

May you refuse thoughts that weaken you, thoughts that take your eyes off of God.

May you instead embrace thoughts that are true based on God's great love for you.

May you refuse to speak about your life apart from faith.

May you instead embrace faith, speak life, and choose life every single moment of every single day.

Rest well.

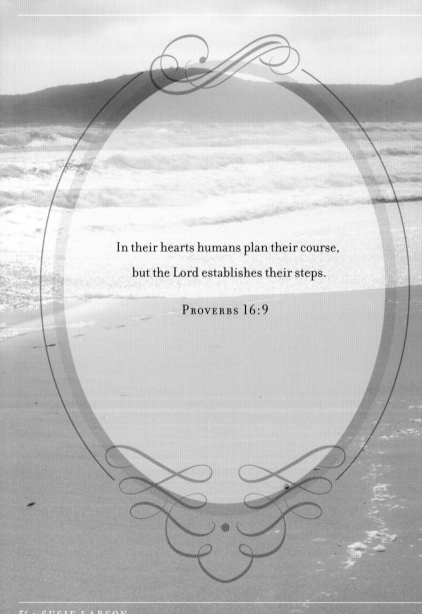

In their hearts humans plan their course,

but the Lord establishes their steps.

PROVERBS 16:9

# *Walk in Faith*

May you—in spite of your fears—walk boldly
in faith.

May you know in the depths of your being how
"for you" God is!

May you embrace your sense of
purpose with tenacity and hope.

And may you walk so intimately with
God that He is able to divinely inter-
rupt your day whenever it suits Him.

Have a blessed, faith-filled day!

The LORD
will fight for you;
you need only
to be still.

EXODUS 14:14

# The Battle Is the Lord's

As you lie down to sleep, may the Lord himself rise up and fight for you!

May He draw by His Spirit your loved ones who do not love Him.

May He bring the breakthrough where there's only been a roadblock.

May you remember this day and every day that the battle is the Lord's!

Rest, knowing God fights for you!

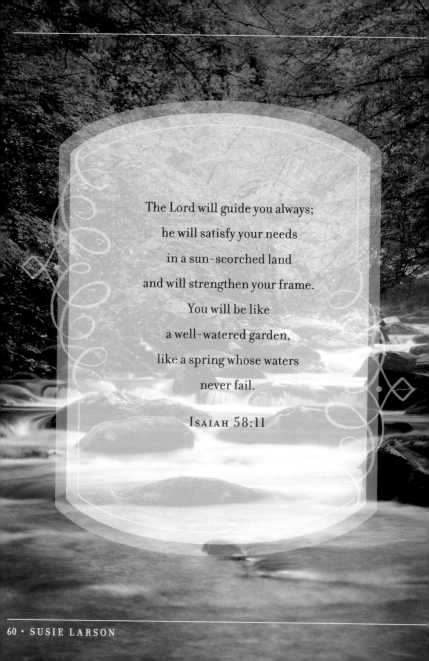

The Lord will guide you always;

he will satisfy your needs

in a sun-scorched land

and will strengthen your frame.

You will be like

a well-watered garden,

like a spring whose waters

never fail.

Isaiah 58:11

# Fresh Favor and Perspective

May God Himself release fresh faith and perspective into your
soul today!

May He strengthen your frame and establish your steps.

May He surround you with good friends who fear God
and who love you.

May He give you fresh vision for your future
and divine wisdom for stewarding your "now"
moments.

May the song in your heart ring louder than the
enemy's threats and accusations.

There is no one like our God and there is nothing like His love for you!

Walk blessed today, because you are!

Each time [the Lord] said,
"My grace is all you need.
My power works best in
weakness." So now I am glad to
boast about my weaknesses, so
that the power of Christ
can work through me.

2 CORINTHIANS 12:9 NLT

# Abounding Grace

May you—in spite of your mistakes and missteps—see how God's love and provision more than cover you.

May you—in your weakness—experience abounding grace that makes you divinely strong.

Where you've experienced loss and brokenness, may you know healing, wholeness, and redemption.

Your Redeemer is for you and He is strong.

Sleep well tonight.

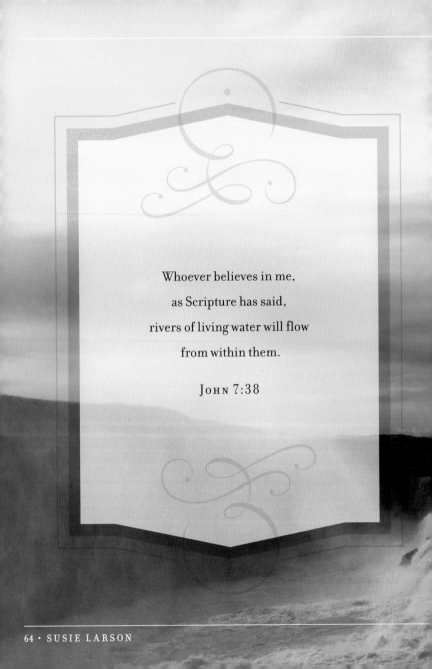

Whoever believes in me,
as Scripture has said,
rivers of living water will flow
from within them.

JOHN 7:38

# A Glimpse of Glory

May God part the heavens and give you a glimpse of how
He sees you.

May He open up your eyes so you can see how much He
loves you.

May He awaken your soul so you'll know healing and
assurance like you've never known before. And may
His love pour in and through you like a river
of living water.

You're connected to the supernatural Source of
power—the Most High God.

May your understanding of what you possess in
Him increase exponentially today!

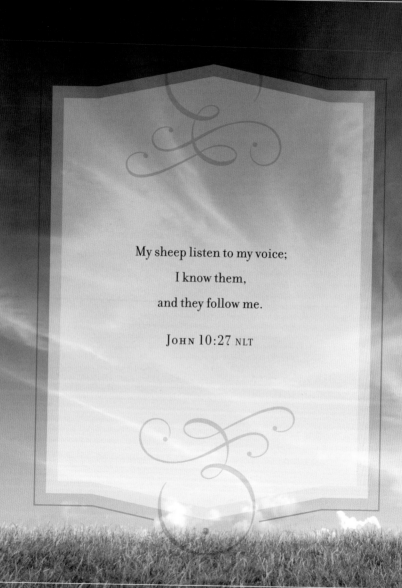

My sheep listen to my voice;

I know them,

and they follow me.

JOHN 10:27 NLT

# Hearing God's Voice

May God give you Spirit-eyes to see the blessing in your battles.

May He give you Spirit-ears to hear His voice above all others.

May He give you a heart of faith to cling to His promises instead of your fears.

May you refuse to live beneath your spiritual privilege and instead live the other-worldly life He has offered you. You are so precious to Him!

Rest in His promises.

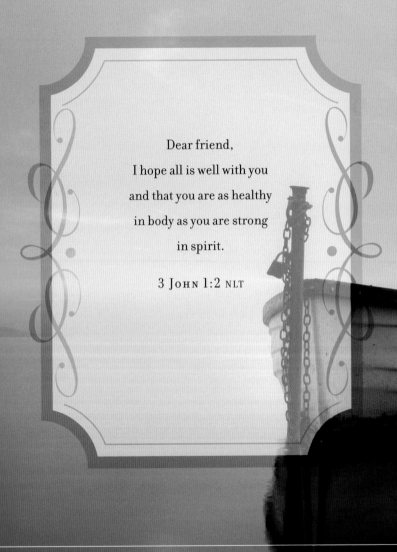

Dear friend,
I hope all is well with you
and that you are as healthy
in body as you are strong
in spirit.

3 John 1:2 NLT

# Healed, Strong, and Whole

May Jesus Himself lift you up and make you strong.

May He heal those hidden areas that surface
time and time again.

May He bring wholeness and health to your mind, body,
and spirit.

May He strengthen you and fill you with faith so you'll dare
to take the risks He puts before you.

May you take time in His presence so you'll remember how
strong and mighty He is. And may your day be filled with
sacred moments that remind you just how precious
you are to Him.

You are so dear to His heart.

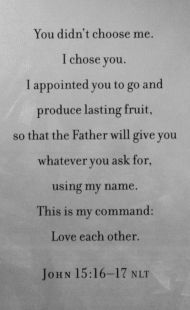

You didn't choose me.
I chose you.
I appointed you to go and
produce lasting fruit,
so that the Father will give you
whatever you ask for,
using my name.
This is my command:
Love each other.

John 15:16–17 NLT

# An Eternal Perspective

As you wrap up your
day, may God grace
you with an eternal
perspective.

Where there's only
been disappoint-
ment, may you trust
God's divine appointment and timing.

Where there's been discouragement, may He inspire new courage to stand strong.

Where there's been whining and griping, may you find
a new song to sing and new reasons for thanksgiving.

May He break through the clouds so you'll see just
how blessed you are.

Sleep well.

Don't worry about anything;

instead, pray about everything.

Tell God what you need,

and thank him for all he has done.

Then you will experience God's peace,

which exceeds anything

we can understand.

His peace will guard your hearts and

minds as you live in Christ Jesus.

PHILIPPIANS 4:6–7 NLT

# *Springtime Expectancy*

May God Himself put springtime in your soul.

May you live today with expectancy that He's doing a new thing in your midst!

May you refuse worry, release your cares, and remember His promises. He'll make a way where there seems to be no way.

Have a faith-filled, expectant day today!

Unless the LORD builds the house,
the builders labor in vain.
Unless the LORD watches over the city,
the guards stand watch in vain.
In vain you rise early
and stay up late,
toiling for food to eat—
for he grants sleep to
those he loves.

PSALM 127:1–2

# Love in Action

May the Lord bring fulfillment to your work, hilarity to your play, depth to your prayers, and kindness to your words.

May He inspire perspective, conviction, and compassion to change the world.

And tonight, may He grant blessed and sweet sleep.

I place before you Life and Death,

Blessing and Curse.

Choose life so that you and your children

will live. And love God, your God,

listening obediently to him, firmly embracing

him. Oh yes, he is life itself,

a long life settled on the soil that God,

your God, promised to give your ancestors,

Abraham, Isaac, and Jacob.

DEUTERONOMY 30:19–20 THE MESSAGE

# Choose Life

When the enemy tries to bait you into discouragement, may you instead take your courageous stand in Christ Jesus.

When the devil tries to seduce you into despair, may you instead walk through the door of hope God has provided for you.

When you're tempted to walk down jealousy's path, may you instead embrace your own beautiful purpose and take the high road God has set before you.

There's a best place for your feet today.

Choose life today!

If God is for us,

who can be against us?

He who did not spare his own Son,

but gave him up for us all—

how will he not also, along with him,

graciously give us all things? . . .

No, in all these things

we are more than conquerors

through him who loved us.

ROMANS 8:31–32, 37

# Gritty Faith

May the Lord himself establish you in His best purposes for you.

May He strengthen you with holy conviction and gritty faith to climb every mountain He's assigned to you.

May He increase your capacity to love and encourage others.

And when the enemy rises up against you, may you see with your own eyes how God fights for you.

You're on the winning side.

You can rest.

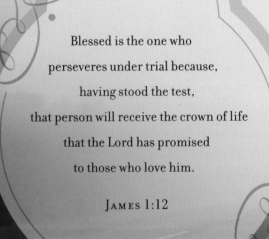

Blessed is the one who

perseveres under trial because,

having stood the test,

that person will receive the crown of life

that the Lord has promised

to those who love him.

JAMES 1:12

## Do Not Quit

May the Lord give you gritty perseverance
to stay the course and continue onward.

May He give you moments of
replenishment that refresh your soul
and renew your perspective.

May He use your wisdom and experience
to bless those who now walk where you've
walked. And may He inspire fresh faith to
trust Him in this place He has you.

You're blessed to be a blessing.

You're under His charge and under His care.

Walk on in faith today!

The LORD is my shepherd;

I have all that I need.

He lets me rest in green meadows;

he leads me beside peaceful streams.

He renews my strength.

He guides me along right paths, bringing

honor to his name.

PSALM 23:1–3

# *Rest for the Weary*

May God lead you beside still waters and provide
rest for your weary soul.

May He set you right where your thinking is wrong.

May He give you faith to embrace the *you*
He's making you to be.

And may He give you wisdom to stand and fight when
your promised land depends on it.

You have everything you need in Him.

May God's rich blessings be yours tonight.

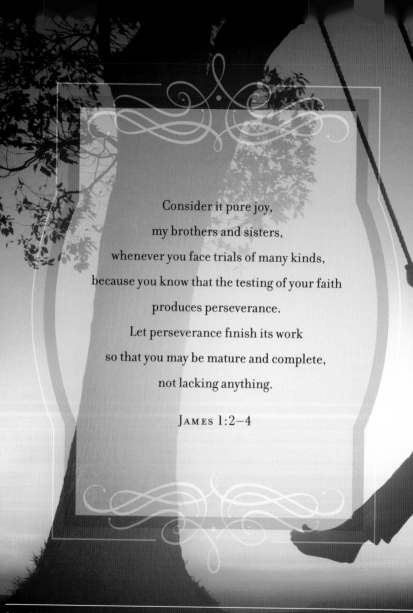

Consider it pure joy,

my brothers and sisters,

whenever you face trials of many kinds,

because you know that the testing of your faith

produces perseverance.

Let perseverance finish its work

so that you may be mature and complete,

not lacking anything.

JAMES 1:2–4

# *Joy and Strength*

May God Himself fill you with pure joy amidst your trials.

May you understand that He's developing perseverance in you so you'll be mature and complete, lacking in nothing.

May you see the blessing in your battles.

Instead of becoming self-aware and wondering why so many arrows are aimed at you, may you simply become a better warrior.

May you lay hold of the generous amounts of wisdom God has offered you in this place so that when it's all said and done, you're still standing.

Have a great and victorious day.

"No weapon forged against you
will prevail,
and you will refute every tongue
that accuses you.
This is the heritage of the servants
of the Lord,
and this is their vindication from me,"
declares the Lord.

Isaiah 54:17

# Equipped for Victory

(Speak this over yourself):

I am loved, called, and chosen.

I am rich in every way and generous on every occasion.

I'm anointed, appointed, equipped, and enabled by the power of God that works mightily within me! No weapon formed against me will prosper and no enemy scheme against me will succeed.

I live, breathe, and serve powerfully under the shelter of the Most High God. Amen.

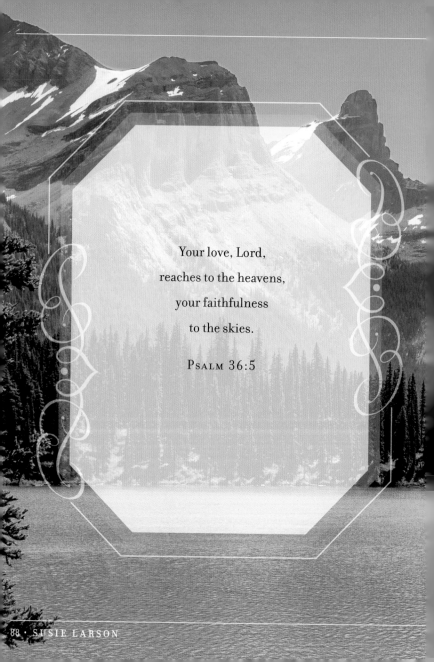

Your love, Lord,

reaches to the heavens,

your faithfulness

to the skies.

PSALM 36:5

# Confident in God

May your whole life align with God's best purposes for you!

May you pray in a way that reveals your solid belief in His faithfulness.

May you speak in a way that reflects the
power of His Word
mightily at work within you.

And may you walk on water when He bids you to come so that others will see and believe that God still moves on the earth today.

A blessed and faith-filled day to you!

We know that God causes
everything to work together
for the good of those who love God
and are called
according to his purpose for them.

ROMANS 8:28 NLT

# God Is Working for You

As the day draws to a close, may
you embrace God's grace,
trusting He'll fill every gap.

Instead of being unsettled
by your imperfections, may
you be undone by Jesus'
perfect love for you.

Instead of fretting over your missteps,
rejoice that He never left your side
today.

Scoop this day into your hand and lift it up as an offering to the
One who moves mountains and ministers miracles with every
little handful we give Him.

He's a miracle-working God and He loves you.

She watches over the affairs

of her household and

does not eat the bread of idleness.

PROVERBS 31:27

# Motivated and Purposeful

May you be motivated to exercise, organize, and prioritize.

May you embrace the grace to tend to the important things so they don't become urgent things.

May God bless you with focus, clarity, and inspiration to live an anointed and purposeful life starting today.

And may abundant grace and startling clarity be yours today!

I have not stopped thanking God for you.

I pray for you constantly,

asking God, the glorious Father

of our Lord Jesus Christ,

to give you spiritual wisdom

and insight so that

you might grow in

your knowledge of God.

Ephesians 1:16–17 NLT

# A Personal Revival

May you experience a personal revival
that forever marks the way you walk with
God.

May your loved ones encounter Him in
ways that change how they pray, what they
say, and how they live.

May God move on your prayers in ways that compel you to pray
more specifically,
with greater fer-
vency, and with
increasing faith.

Though the enemy
is working overtime, he runs scared when God steps in.

May God move mightily in our midst in the
days ahead!

Have a blessed and faith-filled evening!

"For I know the plans I have for you,"
declares the Lord, "plans to prosper you
and not to harm you, plans to give you hope
and a future. Then you will call on me
and come and pray to me, and I will listen
to you. You will seek me and find me
when you seek me with all your heart."

JEREMIAH 29:11–13

# Remember and Dream With God

May you pause today, look back over your shoulder, and remember the ways God has been good to you, has come through for you, and has kept His word to you.

May you look ahead in faith with expectancy, as you get a sense of the land He wants you to claim.

May faith rise up within you as you take your first steps in that direction.

And may you embrace a renewed resolve to walk intimately with the One who loves you and has a beautiful plan for your life.

He deserves some sacred space in your day today!

Blessings to you.

Take my yoke upon you.

Let me teach you,

because I am humble and gentle at heart,

and you will find rest for your souls.

For my yoke is easy to bear,

and the burden I give you is light.

MATTHEW 11:29–30 NLT

# *Let God Carry the Load*

May you have the presence of mind to cherish every second with the ones you love.

May you make time for fun, for rest, and for reflection.

May you plan time in your schedule not to have plans, and see what happens.

May you come to know—on a whole new level—that much more rests on God's shoulders than on yours.

And may you learn to enjoy the journey because His yoke is easy and His burden is light.

And He's crazy in love with you.

Sleep well tonight.

Do not throw away
your confidence; it will be
richly rewarded.

HEBREWS 10:35

# Breakthrough and Renewal

May your persistent prayers pay off and may the burdens that have plagued you suddenly feel like a light and easy yoke.

May this "suddenly" breakthrough come quickly.

May God grant you a fresh revelation of His love and a fresh outpouring of grace to not only face the day but to conquer it valiantly.

And may you experience increasing joy because you believe— beyond a shadow of a doubt—that God has amazing things planned for you! Have a GREAT day!

He will cover you
with his feathers.
He will shelter you
with his wings.
His faithful promises are
your armor and protection.

PSALM 91:4 NLT

# Covered by God

As you get ready to crawl into bed tonight, may you hand Jesus your worries and grab hold of His peace and perspective.

May you lay down your judgments and hold close His fresh mercies.

As you slip under the covers, remember you're not under your circumstances, you are under the shadow of His wings.

Take hold of what you possess in Him, and sleep well.

For no word from God

will ever fail.

LUKE 1:37

# Fresh, Unfailing Mercies

May God Himself wrap you up in His new mercies this day!

Where you've known angst, may He give you awe-inspiring wonder.

Where you've known heartbreak, may He bring healing, deliverance, and a supernatural breakthrough.

May He help you blow the dust off your dreams and lift them up as a possibility once again. With God all things are possible. May you learn to pray from that beautiful truth.

Be lifted up today. He's got you!

So shall they fear the name of the LORD
from the west,
and His glory from the rising of the sun;
when the enemy comes in like a flood,
the Spirit of the LORD will lift up
a standard against him.

ISAIAH 59:19 NKJV

# Coming Against the Enemy

May God give you faith to put fear under your feet.

May you know that for every way the enemy comes against you, the Lord has a promise to bless you to help you stand strong.

May you fix your eyes on Jesus and set your heart on His Word.

Know this: When the enemy comes in like a flood, the Lord will raise up a standard against him!

Trust in God and sleep in peace tonight.

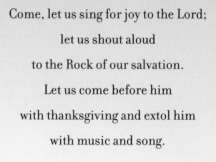

Come, let us sing for joy to the Lord;

let us shout aloud

to the Rock of our salvation.

Let us come before him

with thanksgiving and extol him

with music and song.

Psalm 95:1–2

# Worship Wins the Day

May you awaken to the divine power of a grateful heart.

May you know there's victory in praise and breakthrough in thanksgiving!

When you stomp your feet, raise your hands, and sing a song of praise, the enemy scurries away, covers his ears, and his plans come to nothing.

With God on your side, you have all you need to win your battles and grow in love.

Sing a song of praise today even while you wait for your breakthrough!

A blessed day to you.

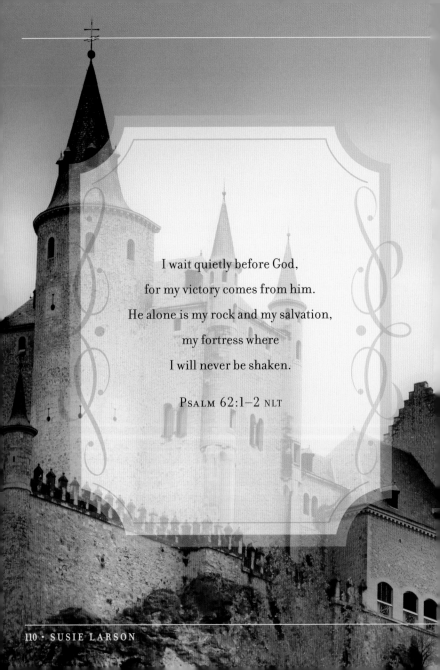

I wait quietly before God,

for my victory comes from him.

He alone is my rock and my salvation,

my fortress where

I will never be shaken.

PSALM 62:1–2 NLT

# *He Is Faithful*

May God open the heavens, break through the clouds, and deliver the answer you've been waiting for.

May He shore up your faith, strengthen your heart, and overwhelm you with His grace.

May your soul know a peaceful assurance like it's never known before.

May you believe from deep within that God is with you, for you, and will never let you go.

He is mighty to save.

Rest well tonight.

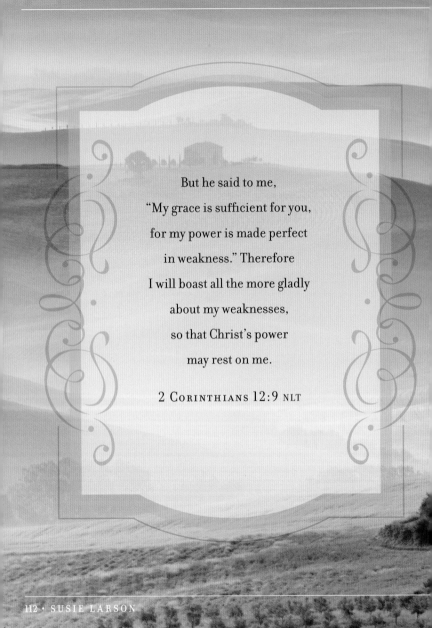

But he said to me,
"My grace is sufficient for you,
for my power is made perfect
in weakness." Therefore
I will boast all the more gladly
about my weaknesses,
so that Christ's power
may rest on me.

2 CORINTHIANS 12:9 NLT

# *There's a Place for You*

When you feel like you don't fit in, may you walk in faith because you have a place at the Table of Grace.

When you feel like you're just not enough, may you remember that His Enough is more than enough for you.

When you trip up and fall short, remember that He stoops down to make you great.

And when you don't feel victorious, remember that you're already seated with Christ because He won the victory for you.

Have a great day!

Confess your sins to each other

and pray for each other

so that you may be healed.

The earnest prayer of

a righteous person

has great power and

produces wonderful results.

JAMES 5:16

# Right Place, Right Time

May God stir up fresh faith in your heart.

May your prayers be packed with power and your words seasoned with love.

May God give you divine instinct so you're always in the right place at the right time.

And may He open a door for you no man can close.

Sleep deeply, sleep well!

It is good to praise the Lord
and make music to your name,
O Most High, proclaiming your love
in the morning
and your faithfulness at night.

Psalm 92:1–2

# Prayer Changes Things

May you begin to see with Spirit eyes all the ways God is moving because of your prayers.

May you begin to hear with heavenly ears the song heaven sings over you.

May you begin to know—on a deeper level—how important and precious your faith is to God.

And may you begin to know that God's promises are absolutely true, and live accordingly.

You couldn't be more loved if you tried. He's sold on you.

A happy and blessed day to you!

As for God, his way is perfect:

The LORD's word is flawless;

he shields all who take refuge in him.

For who is God besides the LORD?

And who is the Rock except our God?

It is God who arms me with strength

and keeps my way secure.

He makes my feet like the feet of a deer;

he causes me to stand on the heights.

2 SAMUEL 22:31–34

# *The Rock*

May God's love and truth bring clarity and purpose to your life.

May His strength steady your steps.

May His compassion open your eyes and may
His conviction make your heart beat strong.

May His kingdom come and His will be
done in and through you.

Rest in His truth.

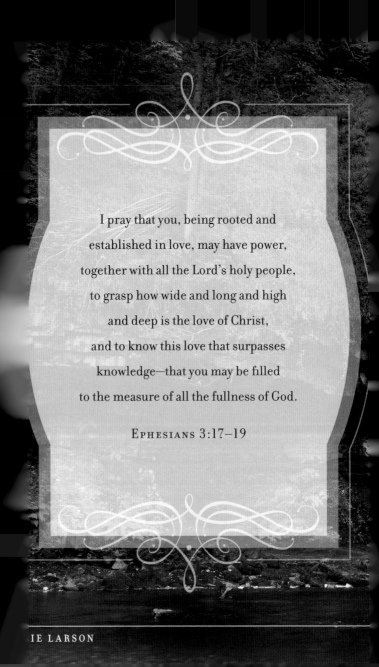

I pray that you, being rooted and
established in love, may have power,
together with all the Lord's holy people,
to grasp how wide and long and high
and deep is the love of Christ,
and to know this love that surpasses
knowledge—that you may be filled
to the measure of all the fullness of God.

Ephesians 3:17–19

# Filled to Overflowing

May you experience increase in every way.

May your capacity to know the heights of God's love grow exponentially.

May your understanding of the depths of His faithfulness grow continually.

May your belief in your divine value deepen tremendously.

And, in the days ahead, may your willingness to trust God with every detail of your life change profoundly.

You are deeply loved, deeply called, and profoundly cared for. May you live out of this truth!

Walk in humble confidence today.

May the God of your father help you;

may the Almighty bless you with

the blessings of the heavens above,

and blessings of the watery depths below,

and blessings of the breasts and womb.

May the blessings of your father surpass

the blessings of the ancient mountains,

reaching to the heights of the eternal hills.

May these blessings rest on the head of Joseph,

who is a prince among his brothers.

GENESIS 49:25–26 NLT

# Grateful Living

May you wrap your arms around the ones you love,
    look them in the eyes, and tell them
    how much you treasure them.

    May you look around and take notice
    of all the blessings you'd miss
    if they went away tomorrow.

    When you're tempted to indulge in
    melancholy or discontentment, may
    you instead jump up, raise your hands,
    and thank God for His daily and divine
    intervention in your life.

    May your humble gratitude give you keen
spiritual insight and restful peace.

Now you have every
spiritual gift you need
as you eagerly wait for
the return of our Lord Jesus Christ.
He will keep you strong to the end
so that you will be free
from all blame on the day
when our Lord Jesus Christ returns.

1 Corinthians 1:7–8 NLT

# Free to Be You

May you find a new freedom in being the YOU God created you to be!

May you be comfortable in your own skin, excited about your own story, and at peace with your own past because Christ has redeemed every part of you.

May you break free from condemnation, may you walk away from toxic influences, and may you put fear under your feet.

Let faith fill your heart. Do not give people the power that belongs to God alone.

He loves you.

He is strong.

And He'll keep you strong till the end.

Have a faith-filled day today!

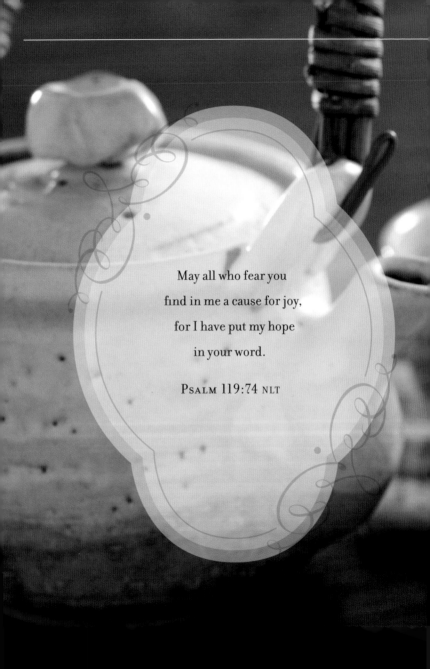

May all who fear you

find in me a cause for joy,

for I have put my hope

in your word.

Psalm 119:74 NLT

## *From Fearful to Joyful*

May God surround you with His tender mercies and encompass you with a fresh revelation of His love.

May He keep you hidden away from toxic people and strengthen your healthy relationships.

May He bless you with a new friend who sees what He sees in you.

And may you rest tonight knowing He'll be there to greet you in the morning.

Sleep deeply, sleep well.

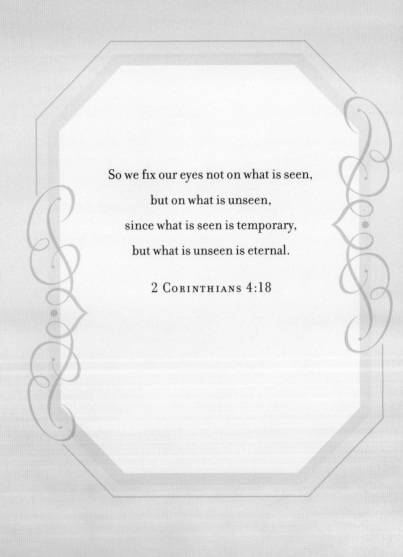

So we fix our eyes not on what is seen,

but on what is unseen,

since what is seen is temporary,

but what is unseen is eternal.

2 Corinthians 4:18

# Release Your Cares

May God Himself surround you with His tender mercies and grace today.

May He heal your soul so you can live by faith.

Where you once reacted out of your insecurities, may you respond in faith knowing you possess all in Christ.

Where you once white-knuckled your worries, may you release every care to Him and lift your hands in praise.

You are not made for this world. You are only passing through.

Live as the divinely loved and called soul you are!

It is for freedom
that Christ has set us free.
Stand firm, then,
and do not let yourselves
be burdened again by
a yoke of slavery.

GALATIANS 5:1

# Freedom in Christ

It is *for* freedom that Christ has set you free.

May you refuse to be subject to any yoke of slavery—slavery to sin, fear, legalism, or striving.

May you rest in the knowledge that Jesus paid it all so that you could walk free and whole.

May you boldly live the abundant, fruitful life He had in mind from the beginning.

You are everything to Him.

May the God of hope fill you with all joy
and peace as you trust in him,
so that you may overflow with hope
by the power of the Holy Spirit.

ROMANS 15:13

# Simplify and Refresh

May God inspire you to tackle a project you've been putting off.

May He motivate you to clean out the clutter and simplify your surroundings.

May He refresh your weary soul and renew your tired mind. And in every way, may your soul be restored, your mind renewed, and your spirit at peace.

He leads you by still waters; follow Him there.

Be revived and refreshed this day!

It is good to give thanks to the LORD,

to sing praises to the Most High.

It is good to proclaim your unfailing love

in the morning, your faithfulness in

the evening. . . . You thrill me, LORD,

with all you have done for me!

I sing for joy because of

what you have done.

PSALM 92:1–2, 4 NLT

## *Praises to the Most High*

May you raise your arms and praise God for His faithfulness to you.

May you open your hands and receive what He so lovingly wants to give.

May you look past your circumstances and see Jesus who reigns over all.

And may you move forward in faith, knowing all things are possible through Him.

A blessed and restful night to you!

I pray that the eyes of your heart
may be enlightened in order that
you may know the hope
to which he has called you,
the riches of his glorious
inheritance in his holy people.

EPHESIANS 1:18

# What's Best for Your Soul

May God divinely motivate you to do what's best for your soul.

If it's spring cleaning, may you clean with a new song in your heart.

If it's reading a book, may you find one that rocks your world.

If it's sharing what you've learned, may you speak with God's passion and power.

And if it's giving, may you give generously and joyfully, believing God will resupply and then some.

Your journey is unique to you.

Listen for His voice and do what He says. God's best is your best!

I don't mean to say that I have already achieved these things or that I have already reached perfection. But I press on to possess that perfection for which Christ Jesus first possessed me. No, dear brothers and sisters, I have not achieved it, but I focus on this one thing: Forgetting the past and looking forward to what lies ahead, I press on to reach the end of the race and receive the heavenly prize for which God, through Christ Jesus, is calling us.

PHILIPPIANS 3:12–14 NLT

# A Heavenly Aim

May you embrace the grace to leave your past in God's hands.

May you have the grit to face down your fears.

May you have the gumption to go after your God-given dreams.

And may you see God's glory shining over every part of your life.

He gives good gifts to His children.

Rest well tonight.

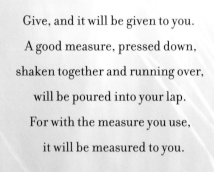

Give, and it will be given to you.
A good measure, pressed down,
shaken together and running over,
will be poured into your lap.
For with the measure you use,
it will be measured to you.

LUKE 6:38

# Sow Generously

May you choose joy this day!

May you look for and count your many blessings.

May you sow generously for a future harvest.

May you trust God with the seeds you have in the ground.

And may you add faith to every deed, knowing that God multiplies what we sow in faith.

Have an abundantly joyful day today!

But the godly will flourish
like palm trees and grow strong
like the cedars of Lebanon.
For they are transplanted to
the LORD's own house.
They flourish in the courts
of our God.
Even in old age they will
still produce fruit;
they will remain vital and green.

PSALM 92:12–14 NLT

# A Fruitful Life

May you walk with a new
confidence that in Christ you
are prized, loved, accepted,
called, equipped, and sent
out to change the world.

You lack no good thing!

And tonight, may you rest
in His shadow. He's got you.

Blessed are the meek,

for they will inherit the earth.

MATTHEW 5:5

# Humility and Tenacity

May God fill you with strength and power to embrace His grace this very hour.

May you humble yourself before Him so that He may lift you up and bless you before a watching world.

May you embrace a humble, teachable heart while maintaining tenacious and ferocious faith.

May you bow low when He speaks and rise up when He tells you to move.

Our God is King, and He moves mightily in and through His people.

Live expectantly today!

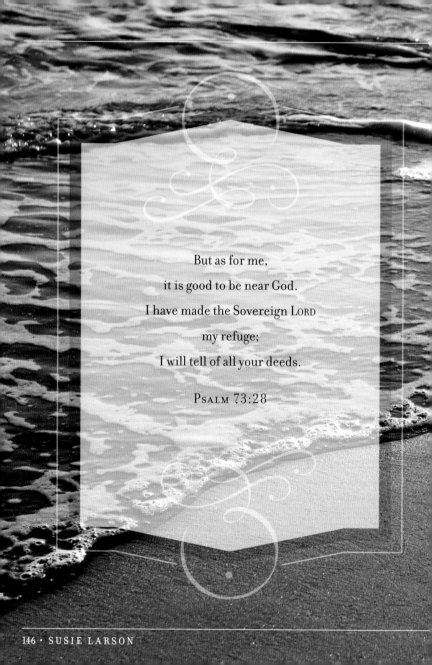

But as for me,

it is good to be near God.

I have made the Sovereign LORD

my refuge;

I will tell of all your deeds.

PSALM 73:28

# *Step-by-Step With God*

May God surround you with a strong sense of His great love for you!

May you live every day with the expectancy that He is moving in your life.

May the Word of God come alive to you in a way you've never experienced.

And may your prayers take on a whole new level of power and faith.

You are His child and He is with you every step of the way.

Be blessed with deep rest this evening.

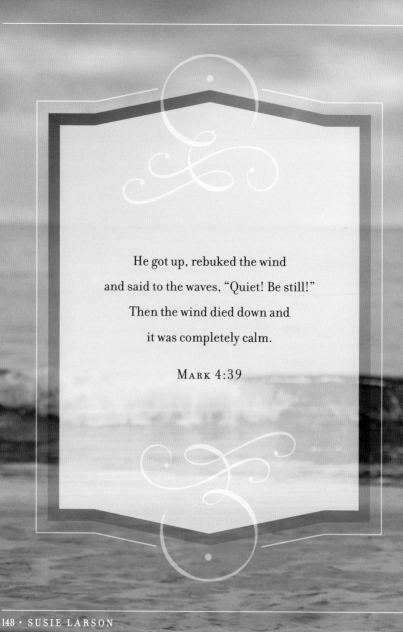

He got up, rebuked the wind
and said to the waves, "Quiet! Be still!"
Then the wind died down and
it was completely calm.

MARK 4:39

# Peace to Your Storm

May Jesus speak peace to your soul and calm to your storm.

May you sense His nearness even when the winds blow.

May you know His joy and strength from the top of your head to the tips your toes.

May the hope He stirs in your heart cause you to live with a holy expectancy and trust that this storm too shall pass.

And in the days ahead, may His very real love for you compel you to dance in the rain before the sun breaks through.

Jesus goes before you, He's got your back, and He's there, just around the bend.

He'll never forsake you.

Trust Him today!

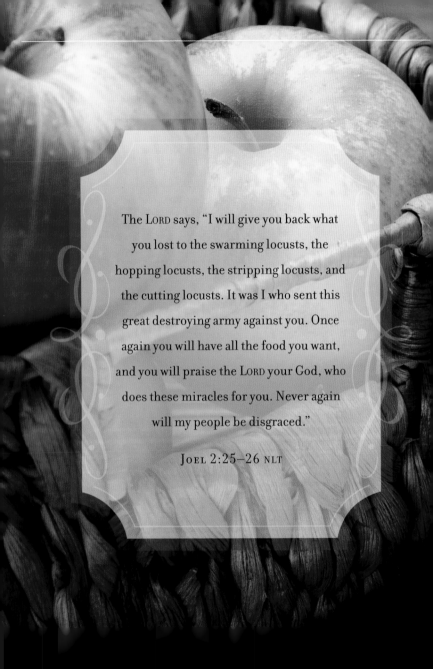

The LORD says, "I will give you back what you lost to the swarming locusts, the hopping locusts, the stripping locusts, and the cutting locusts. It was I who sent this great destroying army against you. Once again you will have all the food you want, and you will praise the LORD your God, who does these miracles for you. Never again will my people be disgraced."

JOEL 2:25–26 NLT

# Your New Future

May God lift you up and heal and restore you fully.

May you see glimpses of His glory everywhere you turn.

May He show you wonders of His love that overwhelm you and make your knees weak.

May He put a new song in your heart and a new dream in your spirit.

May you walk forward unafraid and full of faith that your future will be far greater than your past.

Every valley shall be raised up,

every mountain and hill made low;

the rough ground shall become level,

the rugged places a plain.

And the glory of the Lord will be revealed,

and all people will see it together.

For the mouth of the Lord has spoken.

ISAIAH 40:4–5

## Seated With Christ

No matter if you're in the valley or on a mountain, may you remember most importantly that as a Christ-follower you are seated with Christ in the heavenly realms.

Everything He has is yours.

He has written your name on His hand and holds your desires close to His heart.

Though the elements rage on earth, your footing is secure in Him.

Stay hidden in the shelter of His wing; stay in that place of peace.

May you remember today that nothing can separate you from His powerful, personal love for you.

You're everything to Him.

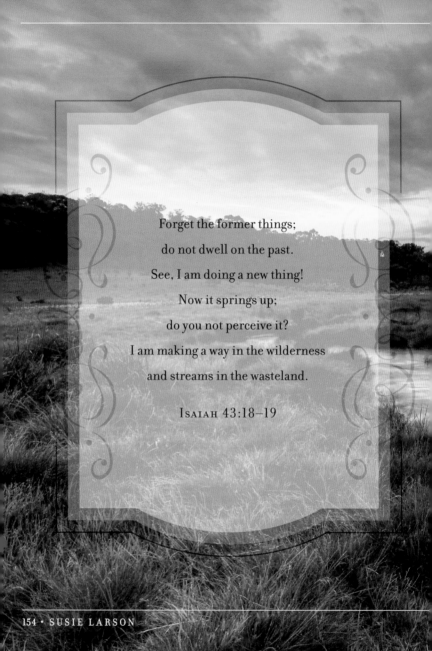

Forget the former things;

do not dwell on the past.

See, I am doing a new thing!

Now it springs up;

do you not perceive it?

I am making a way in the wilderness

and streams in the wasteland.

Isaiah 43:18–19

# A Mighty Move of God

May you have a strong sense of the impossible things God
wants to do in, through, and around you.

May God's dream for you swallow up your unbelief!

May you have faith enough to
put out your buckets and
prepare for rain.

God moves on faith. May He move mightily
because of yours.

And tonight, enjoy restful, faith-filled sleep.

God is mighty to save.

My salvation and my honor

depend on God;

he is my mighty rock,

my refuge.

PSALM 62:7

# Forgiveness and Mercy

May God overwhelm you with grace to forgive those who've hurt you, to forgive yourself for hurting others, and to release the outcomes into His hands.

May He give you the peace to walk forward surrounded by His mercy and held up by His love.

May you look forward expectantly with hope and anticipation because God has the wisdom and the power to make things right.

He redeems, restores, and makes all things new.

Have a great, hope-filled day!

Teach us
to number our days,
that we may gain
a heart of wisdom.

<small>Psalm</small> 90:12

# Sacred Moments

May God help you be fully present with the ones you love.

May He give you discernment not to pass by the sacred moments He supplies.

May He give you faith to believe Him for great things and insight to fully embrace what you already possess in Him.

And may He overwhelm you with a renewed sense of His very personal love for you.

Sleep well tonight.

Teach me to do your will,

for you are my God;

may your good Spirit lead me

on level ground.

Psalm 143:10

# *Don't Give Up*

If you're in a situation you don't want to be in, may you find new strength to stand strong and new resolve to keep walking.

May you earnestly seek God in this place.

May you continue to ask for His strength, insight, and intervention in your life.

May you embrace the expectancy that any day now, your breakthrough will come.

Don't give up hope.

He's got you and you have Him.

You're in this together.

A blessed, faith-filled day to you today!

Don't be afraid—you're not going to be embarrassed. Don't hold back—you're not going to come up short. You'll forget all about the humiliations of your youth, and the indignities of being a widow will fade from memory. For your Maker is your bridegroom, his name, GOD-of-the-Angel-Armies! Your Redeemer is The Holy of Israel, known as God of the whole earth.

ISAIAH 54:4–5 THE MESSAGE

# Tomorrow's Promise

May God expand your territory, enlarge your
vision, and increase your capacity for His
influence in your life.

May you be quick to hear, quick to obey, and quick
to trust Him with every detail of your life.

As you consider His faithfulness today, may you walk
faithfully to your next place of promise tomorrow.

He has been faithful. He *will* be faithful.

Rest assured of that.

But the Lord is with me

like a mighty warrior;

so my persecutors will stumble

and not prevail.

They will fail and be thoroughly disgraced;

their dishonor will never be forgotten.

JEREMIAH 20:11

# Hold Your Ground

In the face of the enemy's lies, taunts, and threats, may you tighten your belt of truth, raise your shield of faith, and hold your ground.

May you refuse to be bullied by your fears or pushed around by your past mistakes.

May you instead look to Jesus, the Author and Finisher of your faith.

May you dare to look ahead to the promised land He's offered you.

You are equipped to win your fear-battle, so press in and press on today!

Through followers of Jesus like
yourselves gathered in churches,
this extraordinary plan of God is
becoming known and talked about even
among the angels! All this is proceeding
along lines planned all along by God
and then executed in Christ Jesus.
When we trust in him, we're free to say
whatever needs to be said, bold to go
wherever we need to go.

Ephesians 3:10–12 The Message

# Secure in Christ

May you understand on a greater
level your secure standing in Christ.

May you approach Him with fresh
boldness and faith, assured of His glad
welcome.

May your prayers move heaven and earth, and
may you remember that everywhere you place
your feet, God's kingdom comes to earth.

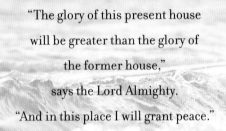

"The glory of this present house
will be greater than the glory of
the former house,"
says the Lord Almighty.
"And in this place I will grant peace."

HAGGAI 2:9

## *Break Free*

May God help you identify the idols in your life—those things that hold you captive, have too much power over you, and keep you from soul freedom.

May you give God the glory He deserves.

May you ascribe to Him the power you once gave to others.

May you thank Him for the future the enemy has threatened to steal from you.

May you walk forward with abundant grace, divine peace, and overwhelming joy because you're profoundly rich in Christ.

Shake the shackles off your feet and praise Him! He's set you free today and every day!

GOD made my life complete when I placed
all the pieces before him. When I got my
act together, he gave me a fresh start.
Now I'm alert to GOD's ways; I don't take
God for granted. Every day I review the
ways he works; I try not to miss a trick.
I feel put back together, and I'm watching
my step. GOD rewrote the text of my life
when I opened the book of my heart
to his eyes.

PSALM 18:20–24 THE MESSAGE

# Living With Expectancy

Jesus is coming soon.

May God open your eyes to see the reality of His kingdom
in your midst, may He open your ears that you may clearly
hear His voice, and may He awaken your heart that you may
passionately and purposefully live for Him.

Live expectantly and sleep well.

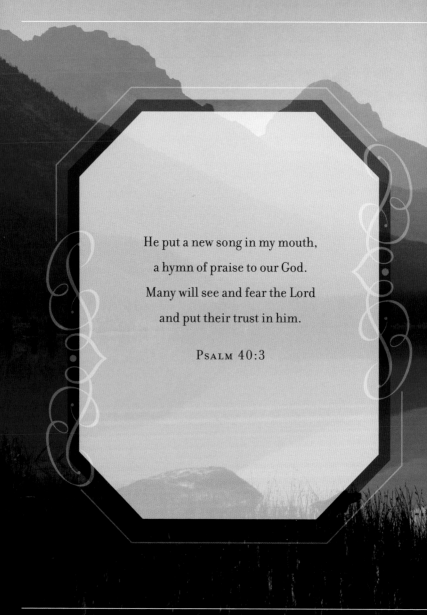

He put a new song in my mouth,

a hymn of praise to our God.

Many will see and fear the Lord

and put their trust in him.

PSALM 40:3

# Spacious Places

May the God of all comfort surround you with His tender mercies and strength.

May He breathe fresh life into your soul and put a new song in your heart.

May He broaden the path beneath your feet and make your footsteps firm.

And may He lead you to a spacious place and answer your heartfelt prayers.

A blessed and beautiful day to you this day!

If you then, being evil,
know how to give good gifts
to your children, how much more
will your heavenly Father
give the Holy Spirit to
those who ask Him!

LUKE 11:13 NKJV

# *Good Gifts*

May you slow down long enough tomorrow to enjoy the sacredness of the present moment.

May God give you plenty of sacred pauses to reflect on His intimate and powerful love for you.

May you enjoy lots of face-to-face encounters with those you love.

May God open your eyes and use you to lift up those bent beneath heavy loads.

May *you* receive the gifts He so lovingly wants to give.

And tonight, may you enjoy deep, refreshing sleep.

Tomorrow's a new day.

I'm absolutely convinced that nothing—nothing living or dead, angelic or demonic, today or tomorrow, high or low, thinkable or unthinkable—absolutely nothing can get between us and God's love because of the way that Jesus our Master has embraced us.

ROMANS 8:38–39
THE MESSAGE

# He Loves and He Restores

May God Himself recover and restore
what the enemy has stolen.

May He heal family rifts, renew tired relationships, and revive
weary faith.

May He lift you up and make you strong.

May He give you wisdom in boundaries and humility in love.

May He show you what's yours and give you grace
to release what isn't.

And may you know beyond a shadow of a doubt that
nothing and no one can separate you from God's love.

Walk in humble, hopeful faith today.

I cry out to God Most High,

to God, who vindicates me.

He sends from heaven and saves me,

rebuking those who hotly pursue me—

God sends forth his love and

his faithfulness.

Psalm 57:2–3

## Mighty to Save

May the Lord continue to fight
for you while you rest in Him.

May He confuse the enemy's schemes against
you.

May He surround you with God-fearing, faithful
friends and strengthen your resolve to live
courageously.

You're on the winning side!

Sleep well.

Turn my eyes away from
worthless things;
preserve my life according to
your word.

PSALM 119:37

## A Fresh Outpouring

May God unleash a
fresh outpouring of
His grace and goodness
over your life.

May He open heaven's doors and
pour out His Spirit in increasing measures.

May He firmly establish you in His highest
and best purposes for you.

May you acquire such a taste for the presence
of God that you're no longer tempted
or distracted by cheap counterfeits and
temporary sources.

He is the one true God and He delights in every
detail of your life.

Have a blessed, power-full day!

Since God chose you to be the holy people
he loves, you must clothe yourselves with
tenderhearted mercy, kindness, humility,
gentleness, and patience. Make allowance for
each other's faults, and forgive anyone
who offends you. Remember, the Lord
forgave you, so you must forgive others.
Above all, clothe yourselves with love,
which binds us all together in perfect
harmony. And let the peace that comes
from Christ rule in your hearts.
For as members of one body you are called
to live in peace. And always be thankful.

COLOSSIANS 3:12–15 NLT

# A Peace Offering

May God give you kindness and grace for those who step
on your toes.

May He give you holy and humble confidence in the presence
of those who misunderstand you.

May He give you love and forgiveness for those who hurt
you and grace for those who miss you completely.

And may His love spill over you till you know that you
are everything to Him.

Sleep well tonight. Walk confidently tomorrow.

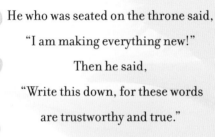

He who was seated on the throne said,

"I am making everything new!"

Then he said,

"Write this down, for these words

are trustworthy and true."

REVELATION 21:5

# God Is Doing a New Thing

May God do a brand-new thing in and through you!

May He break every generational stronghold that keeps you from knowing and experiencing His great love for you.

May He move every mountain that blocks your view of Him.

May He fill every low place with pools of blessing.

And may He restore everything stolen so you can have the life He intended for you from the beginning of time.

Your Redeemer is strong and mighty and loves you deeply.

Live joyfully today!

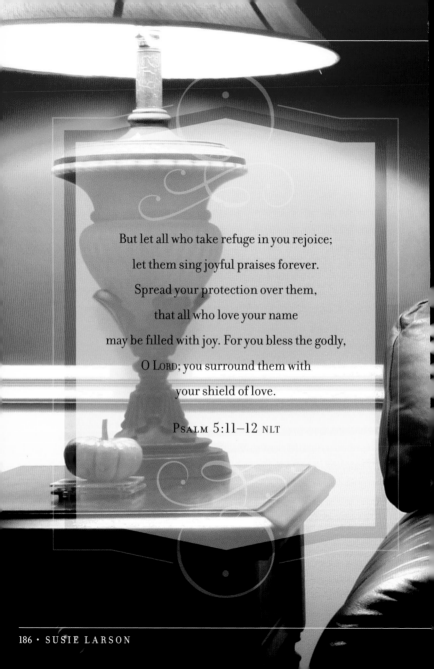

But let all who take refuge in you rejoice;

let them sing joyful praises forever.

Spread your protection over them,

that all who love your name

may be filled with joy. For you bless the godly,

O Lord; you surround them with

your shield of love.

Psalm 5:11–12 NLT

# A Shield of Love

As the day draws to a close and your body gets ready to rest, may your soul awaken to the wonder of God's movement in your life.

He is with you and for you.

His love and favor surround you like a shield.

Listen to His voice as you rest your head on the pillow tonight.

Forsake your worries and fears and cling to faith instead. He's got you in His hands.

Go, walk through the length
and breadth of the land,
for I am giving it to you.

GENESIS 13:17

# Your Next Place of Promise

May the Lord remove every distraction that keeps you from the land He has for you.

May you walk forward in faith to possess it.

May you trust His process as He prepares you to dwell in that land so you can feed on His faithfulness.

Your current battles are training you not only to take the land, but to stand there, fight there, win there, and be fruitful there!

The Lord your God is with you!

Don't worry about anything;
instead, pray about everything.
Tell God what you need,
and thank him for all he has done.
Then you will experience God's peace,
which exceeds anything
we can understand.
His peace will guard your hearts and
minds as you live in Christ Jesus.

Philippians 4:6–7 nlt

# A Thankful Heart

May you set aside your fears, worries, and frustrations,
and pull close the ones you love.

May you notice and give thanks for all that is right
in your world.

May the Lord become especially real to you
in the coming days.

And may you grow in your capacity to thank Him
and trust Him in every single circumstance.

Enjoy sweet rest tonight.

Here is my servant, whom I uphold,

my chosen one in whom I delight;

I will put my Spirit on him,

and he will bring justice to the nations.

Isaiah 42:1

# See Yourself Through His Eyes

May God open your Spirit eyes to see your life, your worth, and your destiny from His point of view.

He's doing a beautiful work in you!

May you open wide your arms and receive His abundant love, His powerful promises, and His moment-by-moment faithfulness.

He will not fail you!

May you live as one who is spoken for, provided for, and deeply loved.

Because you are.

Have a great day!

Always be full of joy in the Lord.

I say it again—rejoice!

Let everyone see that you

are considerate in all you do.

Remember, the Lord is coming soon.

PHILIPPIANS 4:4–5 NLT

# Your Story and God's

May you grow to love and accept the *you* God is making you to be.

May you walk in a new level of grace and gratitude that gives you peace and leaves others encouraged.

May you be more apt to look forward with hope than you are to look back with regret.

May your heart spill over with joy at the very thought of the story God is writing with your life.

Rest in His love.

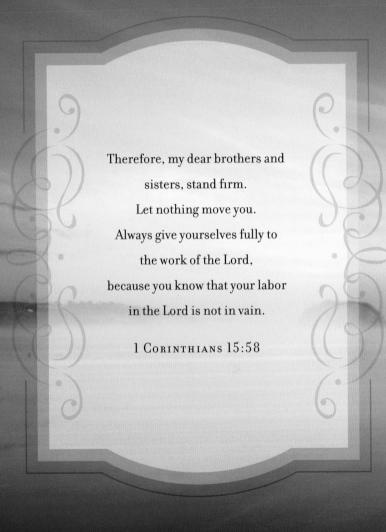

Therefore, my dear brothers and
sisters, stand firm.
Let nothing move you.
Always give yourselves fully to
the work of the Lord,
because you know that your labor
in the Lord is not in vain.

1 Corinthians 15:58

# God Is in Control

May you be assured on a whole new level of how much God loves you and that He's constantly working on your behalf.

May you feel a fresh surge of confidence amidst your circumstances because you know that God is ultimately in control, and nothing escapes His notice.

He only allows battles you can win, and in every one there are treasures and spoils with your name on them.

Live bravely today!

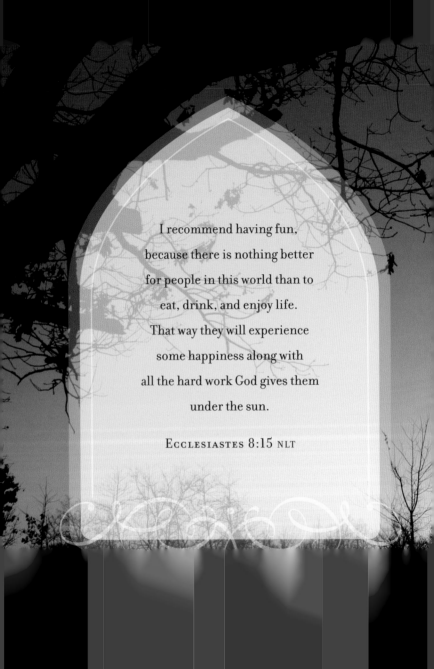

I recommend having fun,
because there is nothing better
for people in this world than to
eat, drink, and enjoy life.
That way they will experience
some happiness along with
all the hard work God gives them
under the sun.

Ecclesiastes 8:15 nlt

# A Full-of-Life Life

May God surprise you with moments of grace and refreshment.

May He bring the long-awaited breakthrough.

May He bless you with sudden belly laughter and watery-eyed joy.

May He give you a gift that you least expect.

And may He inspire you to pray more audaciously than you ever have before.

He is with you and for you.

Lord my God,

I called to you for help,

and you healed me.

PSALM 30:2

## *Give Him Access to You*

May you give God full access
to your story.

May you allow Him to
correct and redirect,
heal and deal, refine and
define, whenever it suits
Him.

He loves you most and
knows what's best for
you at every given moment.
He will lead you in the way you
should go.

May you remember that you're part of
a great story God is writing in the world.

May you trust the Lord's work in your life so He can
use you in ways beyond your wildest dreams.

Lean in and trust Him. He's got you.

Be joyful in hope,
patient in affliction,
faithful in prayer.

ROMANS 12:12

## *Through God's Eyes*

May God give you His perspective on the
things that frustrate you.

May your heart of compassion grow for
those who suffer in unimaginable ways.

May you pray as passionately for them
as you do for yourself.

May God protect you from a small, selfish mind-set.

May He fill you up with thanksgiving and joy for the
freedoms you enjoy!

May He renew your resolve to be a
grateful, humble soul.

And may He use you tomorrow
in ways that surprise and bless
you.

Sweet dreams.

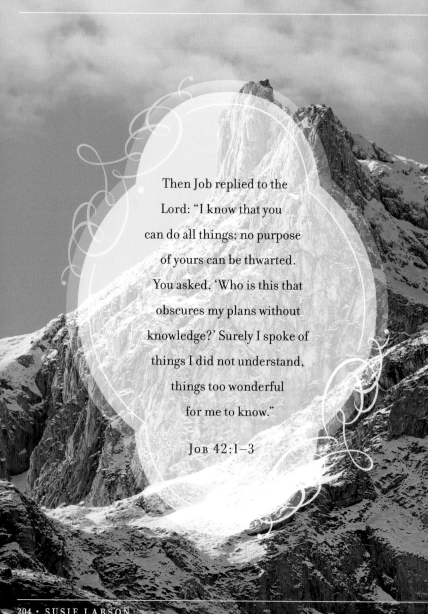

Then Job replied to the
Lord: "I know that you
can do all things; no purpose
of yours can be thwarted.
You asked, 'Who is this that
obscures my plans without
knowledge?' Surely I spoke of
things I did not understand,
things too wonderful
for me to know."

JOB 42:1–3

# Unshakable

In this day of uncertainty, may God give you a faith that cannot be shaken.

When all is in chaos, may you have divine clarity to see God's highest will and divine movement all around you.

May you know peace that passes understanding and pass it on to others.

Stand strong, my friend!

You possess all in Him.

Walk forward unafraid.

The thief comes only

to steal and kill and destroy;

I have come that they may have life,

and have it to the full.

JOHN 10:10

## *Fully Restored*

May God himself restore to you something you lost and never thought you'd get back again.

May He heal a soul wound you thought you'd never get over.

May He pour out an abundance of joy and hope that makes you celebrate before the answer comes.

And may a thriving, rich faith mark your life in every way.

You have access to the Most High God. May you live accordingly.

Rest easy tonight!

Therefore, if anyone is in Christ, the new creation has come: The old has gone, the new is here! All this is from God, who reconciled us to himself through Christ and gave us the ministry of reconciliation.

2 Corinthians 5:17–18

## The New You

May you refuse an anxious heart and embrace a faith-filled one.

May you stomp on your fears and dance because of your dreams.

May you shun the shame of your youth and hold tight your new identity in Christ.

You are not an improved version of your old self. You are something altogether new, profoundly beautiful, and abundantly equipped.

Walk fully in the blessing and purposes of God today.

The LORD is gracious and righteous;

our God is full of compassion.

The LORD protects the unwary;

when I was brought low,

he saved me.

Return to your rest, my soul,

for the LORD has been good to you.

PSALM 116:5–7

# While You Rest

May God work mightily tonight while you rest.

May He move mountains on your behalf.

May He part the waters so you can pass through to your next place of promise.

May you grow in the knowledge of God's love and become a flow-through-account of His blessings to a world in need.

Sleep well tonight.

Why, my soul, are you downcast?

Why so disturbed within me?

Put your hope in God,

for I will yet praise him,

my Savior and my God.

PSALM 42:5

## Trust Him Fully

May you dare to trust in the Lord with your whole heart and not lean on your own understanding.

May you look up and acknowledge Him with every step you take, knowing He'll get you where you need to go.

May you put your hope in Him and not in the approval of man.

God will never disappoint.

He loves you more than you can comprehend.

Trust Him, and soon your eyes will see how good He is.

Blessings on your day today!

Don't you realize that in a race everyone runs,
but only one person gets the prize?
So run to win! All athletes are disciplined in
their training. They do it to win a prize that will
fade away, but we do it for an eternal prize.
So I run with purpose in every step.
I am not just shadowboxing. I discipline my
body like an athlete, training it to do what it
should. Otherwise, I fear that after preaching to
others I myself might be disqualified.

1 Corinthians 9:24–27 NLT

## Purpose in Every Step

May God establish you in His highest and best purposes for you.

May He point out your time-wasters and life-drainers,
and may you have the grit to walk away from them.

May His passion become your passion so that your life
reflects His abundant life plan for you.

And tonight, may your sleep heal and restore you
in every way.

You're treasured and blessed.

Curses chase sinners
while blessings chase
the righteous!

PROVERBS 13:21 TLB

# *Abundantly Blessed*

May abundant grace and profound peace be multiplied
to you in every way.

May countless blessings chase and overtake you, and
may you notice when they do.

May God heal your heart, soul, mind, and body, and
may you approach life with eternity in mind.

May you know the wholeness God always intended for you,
and may your faith be renewed.

Look for Him expectantly today!

Then, because so many people
were coming and going that
they did not even have a chance to eat,
[Jesus] said to them, "Come with me
by yourselves to a quiet place
and get some rest."

MARK 6:31

# A Quiet Place

May you put a high priority on rest and replenishment.

May you make a plan to get away and nourish your soul.

May you do your work with great excellence.

May you take on a challenge that stretches your faith
and increases your dependence on God.

May your work be especially satisfying and
your rest be especially sweet.

Life is good that way.

Bless you!

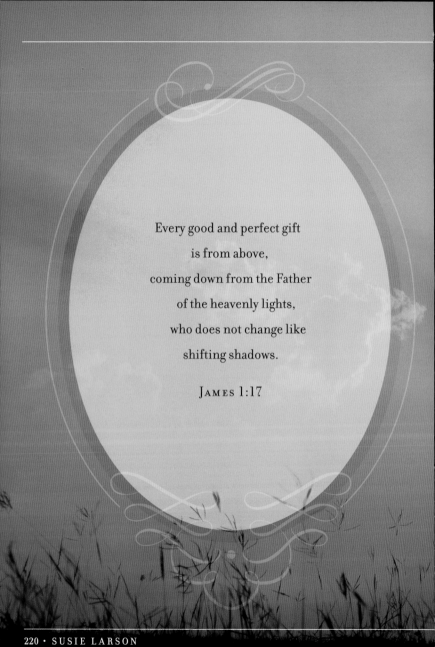

Every good and perfect gift

is from above,

coming down from the Father

of the heavenly lights,

who does not change like

shifting shadows.

JAMES 1:17

# A Playful Moment

May you face today with
a smile and with hopeful
expectancy.

May God surprise you with a
song that speaks to your heart.

May you enjoy a sudden playful
moment and enter in with your
whole heart.

And may you notice that every good
gift in your life comes from
above.

In every season, He gives good
gifts to His children.

A blessed and wonderful day to
you this day!

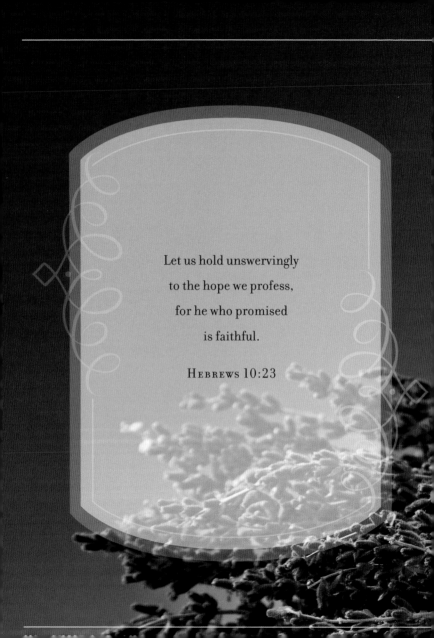

Let us hold unswervingly
to the hope we profess,
for he who promised
is faithful.

HEBREWS 10:23

# A Better Tomorrow

May you find a moment of peace and quiet tonight to thank God for all that is right in your world.

May you have the presence of mind to release your cares and worries to Him.

May you have the gritty faith to grab a firmer grip on His promises to you.

And may you wake up in the morning knowing that you've gained ground even during your sleeping hours because God is always moving on your behalf.

As you entrust your whole self to Him today, He'll get you where you need to go tomorrow.

He is faithful.

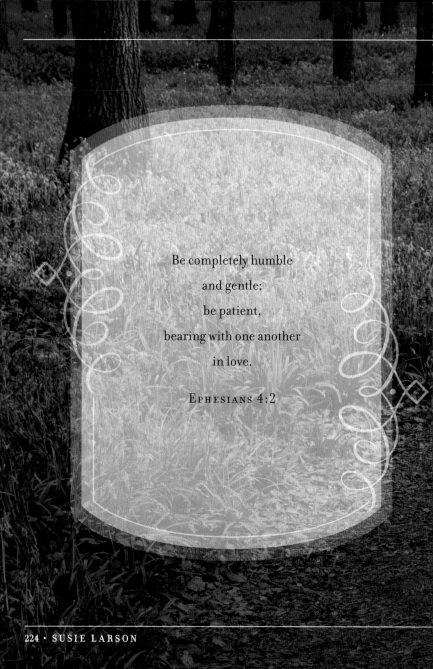

Be completely humble
and gentle;
be patient,
bearing with one another
in love.

Ephesians 4:2

# *Energized and Purposeful*

May God infuse you with divine energy and purpose today.

May He fuel your prayers and sanctify your words.

May He open your eyes to see evidences of His handiwork everywhere you turn.

And may He connect you with people you need to meet, people who need your blessing.

Step forward with authority, confidence, joy, and strength today.

You are mighty in God!

I will sing of your strength, in the morning
I will sing of your love; for you are my fortress,
my refuge in times of trouble.
You are my strength, I sing praise to you;
you, God, are my fortress,
my God on whom I can rely.

PSALM 59:16–17

## You Can Rely on Him

God is your creator, defender, deliverer, and provider.

May He inspire fresh, creative ways to make a living.

May He defend you against the accusations of your critics.

May He deliver you from the schemes of the enemy.

And may He more than provide for all your needs.

He is faithful.

Sleep well in that assurance.

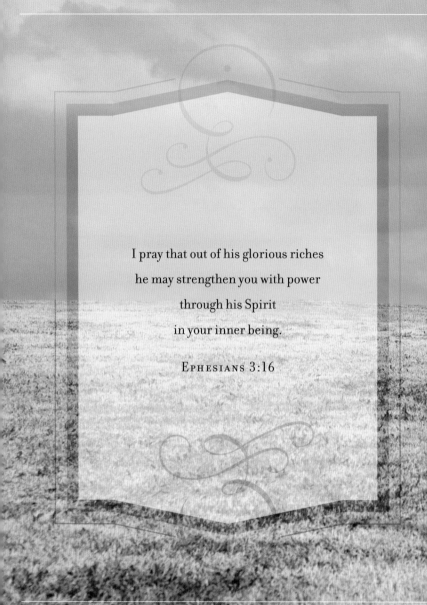

I pray that out of his glorious riches

he may strengthen you with power

through his Spirit

in your inner being.

Ephesians 3:16

# Keep Walking

May you dare to keep walking even though quitting feels like the easier thing to do.

May you dare to look up even though the weight of your burden compels you to look down.

May you dare to dream about the future even though the enemy would love for your past to have the last say.

Keep walking, look up, and dare to dream.

Jesus invites you forward.

Embrace joy today, and don't give up!

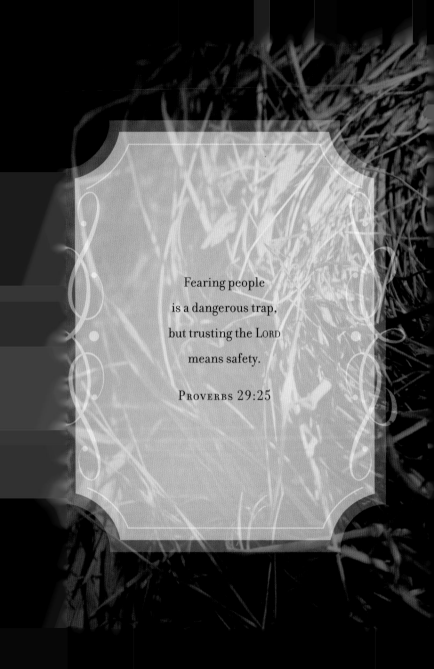

Fearing people
is a dangerous trap,
but trusting the LORD
means safety.

PROVERBS 29:25

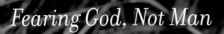

# Fearing God, Not Man

May you be
content to know that
you cannot be all things to all
people; you live to serve an audience of One.

May you love people but keep your hope in God.

May you be willing to take risks with people, but may your sole
trust be in God.

May the power you once gave to others rest solely on God
because He defines, He saves, He provides, and He has the
power to transform.

But you have

God-blessed eyes—eyes that see!

And God-blessed ears—ears that hear!

A lot of people, prophets and

humble believers among them,

would have given anything to see

what you are seeing, to hear

what you are hearing,

but never had the chance.

MATTHEW 13:16–17 THE MESSAGE

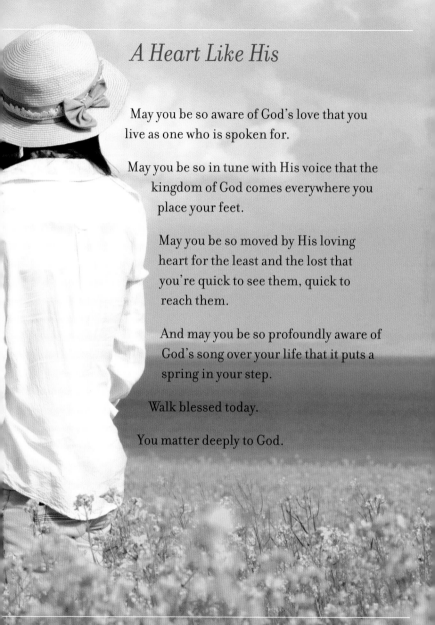

## A Heart Like His

May you be so aware of God's love that you live as one who is spoken for.

May you be so in tune with His voice that the kingdom of God comes everywhere you place your feet.

May you be so moved by His loving heart for the least and the lost that you're quick to see them, quick to reach them.

And may you be so profoundly aware of God's song over your life that it puts a spring in your step.

Walk blessed today.

You matter deeply to God.

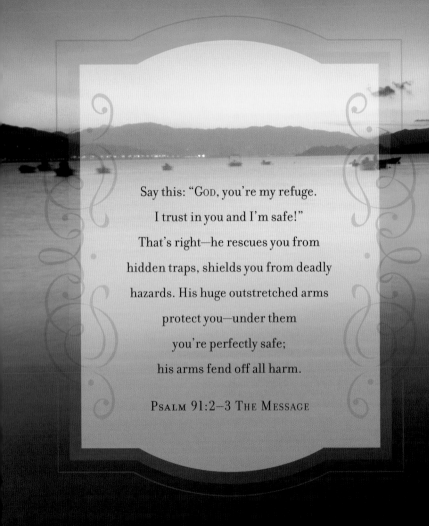

Say this: "God, you're my refuge.

I trust in you and I'm safe!"

That's right—he rescues you from

hidden traps, shields you from deadly

hazards. His huge outstretched arms

protect you—under them

you're perfectly safe;

his arms fend off all harm.

Psalm 91:2–3 The Message

# Following His Lead

May you have the wisdom to run away from temptation
and into the arms of God.

May you know when to run to the battlefield and
when to hide in His shadow.

May you have the courage to run up the mountain and
the guts to step out of the boat when it is required of
you.

May your every step be in step with Him.

Sleep well.

Guard my life,

for I am faithful to you;

save your servant who trusts in you.

You are my God.

PSALM 86:2

# Wisdom to Guard and Guide

May God be exalted in your life today!

May He surround you with fresh mercies and fiery faith, and may His divine wisdom guard and guide you.

May you refuse to dabble in things that make you vulnerable to the enemy's schemes.

May you instead shore up your life, guard your heart, and walk in faith.

You've a great call on your life, and the Lord is mighty in you and through you!

Even before he made the world,

God loved us and chose us

in Christ to be holy

and without fault in his eyes.

EPHESIANS 1:4 NLT

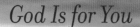

# God Is for You

May God remove every hindrance that keeps you
from knowing His love in a way that changes you.

May He change every circumstance that sends a lying
message to you.

May He highlight every trial He's using to train you
into a warrior.

And may He remind you that all of heaven is on your side.

You are very close to His heart.

Rest in that fact.

And we know that in all things

God works for the good of those

who love him,

who have been called

according to his purpose.

Romans 8:28

# *Awaken Your Faith*

May God ignite fresh faith in you today!

May you pray with clarity, precision, and power.

May you stand on His Word and hold fast to His promises.

May you refuse to fixate on your difficulties, and instead fix your eyes on Jesus—the One who will finish what He started in you.

He is always good, always kind, always true, and He WILL come through for you!

May the Lord overwhelm you with an awakening of faith, hope, and love today.

Look up and be blessed.

Dear friend, I pray that you
may enjoy good health and that
all may go well with you, even as your
soul is getting along well. It gave me great
joy when some believers came and testified
about your faithfulness to the truth,
telling how you continue to walk in it.

3 John 1:2–3

# Abundant Living and Giving

May God prosper you in every way.

May you be emotionally strong and stable,
spiritually deep and thriving, financially free
and generous, socially blessed and a blessing,
and physically fit and healthy.

May God fill in every gap, heal every wound,
and restore everything stolen.

May you live abundantly in every way.

And may you sleep well tonight.

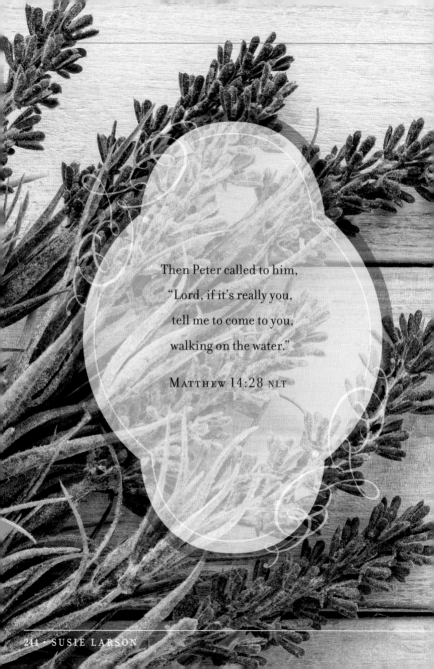

Then Peter called to him,
"Lord, if it's really you,
tell me to come to you,
walking on the water."

MATTHEW 14:28 NLT

# Say Yes

May Jesus bring clarity to His future plans for you.

May you suddenly be assured on a much greater level of
His deep love for you and of His intimate attention to detail.

As He bids you to come, may you let go of what feels safe
to lay hold of the new place He has for you.

He's doing a new thing; don't hang on to the old just because
you know it so well—don't miss out on the invitation.

Take the next faith step in front of you, and have a blessed
and beautiful day!

Now he who supplies seed to the sower
and bread for food will also supply and
increase your store of seed and will enlarge the
harvest of your righteousness.
You will be enriched in every way
so that you can be generous on every occasion,
and through us your generosity will result
in thanksgiving to God.

2 Corinthians 9:10–11

## Harvest Time

May you sow the seeds God has given
you to sow.

May you reap above and beyond anything you
could ever ask or think.

May you know without a doubt your divine call.

And may you open your arms wide and receive
everything God provides along the way.

Have a restful night.

For we live by believing,

not by seeing.

2 Corinthians 5:7 NLT

# Believe, Then See

May you walk by faith and not by sight.

May you live by the promises of God and
not by what your eyes see.

May you—even today—see movement in your
circumstances, glimpses of glory that remind
you your God is very much involved in your life.

He's writing a story, arranging circumstances, moving
in the hearts of people specifically for you. He loves you
that much.

Let your joyful heart testify to your abounding trust in
Him. It'll please God and encourage others!

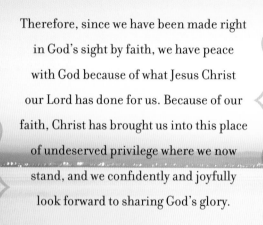

Therefore, since we have been made right in God's sight by faith, we have peace with God because of what Jesus Christ our Lord has done for us. Because of our faith, Christ has brought us into this place of undeserved privilege where we now stand, and we confidently and joyfully look forward to sharing God's glory.

Romans 5:1–2 nlt

# *Valued*

May you learn deeply just how important you are to God.

May you grasp your spiritual wealth and appropriate
your spiritual strength.

May your fears dissolve and your worries vaporize.

May you walk in the full assurance of God's love,
acceptance, and grace.

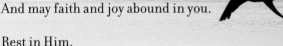

And may faith and joy abound in you.

Rest in Him.

He makes me lie down in green pastures,

he leads me beside quiet waters,

he refreshes my soul.

He guides me along the right paths

for his name's sake.

PSALM 23:2–3

# Still Waters

May the Lord lead you beside still waters and restore your soul.

May He refresh your sense of purpose.

May He renew your love for those He's given to you.

And may He stir in you a hunger to know Him more.

He's only a prayer away.

Embrace a heart at rest this day.

The Scriptures . . . say,
"No eye has seen, no ear has heard,
and no mind has imagined what God
has prepared for those who love him."
But it was to us that God revealed
these things by his Spirit.
For his Spirit searches out everything
and shows us God's deep secrets.

1 Corinthians 2:9–10 nlt

# Beyond Imagination

May you believe that your wildest God-given dreams
can come true.

May you trust Jesus enough to follow Him
through the valley to lay hold of them.

May you be patient and purposeful.

May your selfish ambition die and your
holy ambition arise.

May you lean into your training time so
you'll be strengthened and prepared to stand
in your next place of promise.

Then you'll be poised to change the world.

Tonight, sleep well.

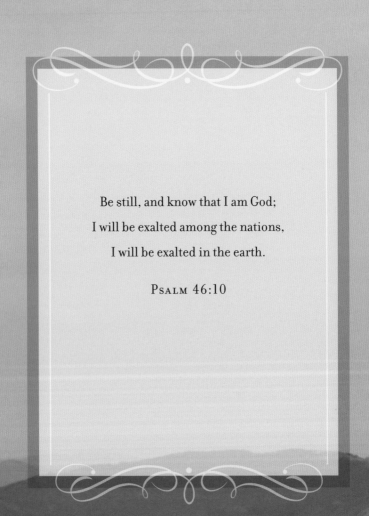

Be still, and know that I am God;

I will be exalted among the nations,

I will be exalted in the earth.

Psalm 46:10

# He's With You

May the Lord reveal His goodness and kindness today.

May you enjoy an intimate and personal relationship with Him. He's right here, with you, and for you.

When you start to strive, may you instead pause, look up, and acknowledge His presence in your life. You're never alone; never out of His care.

Everything He has is yours. You lack no good thing.

Walk in faith today.

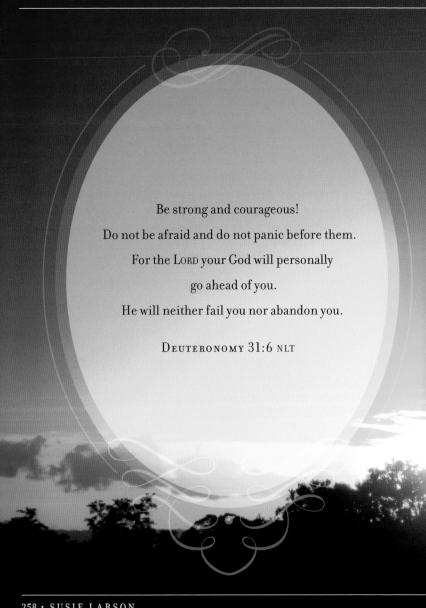

Be strong and courageous!

Do not be afraid and do not panic before them.

For the LORD your God will personally

go ahead of you.

He will neither fail you nor abandon you.

DEUTERONOMY 31:6 NLT

# God Will Lead You

When you are tired and weary, may God give you rest and
a right perspective.

When you are tempted to run ahead on your own, may
He give you divine wisdom to wait on Him.

When your guard is down and you are vulnerable to the
enemy's schemes, may God protect you on every side
and deliver you.

And when you are ready to fly, may He lift you up
and bless you before a watching world.

Take one humble step at a time. He will lead you
to your next place
of promise.

May nourishing sleep
be yours.

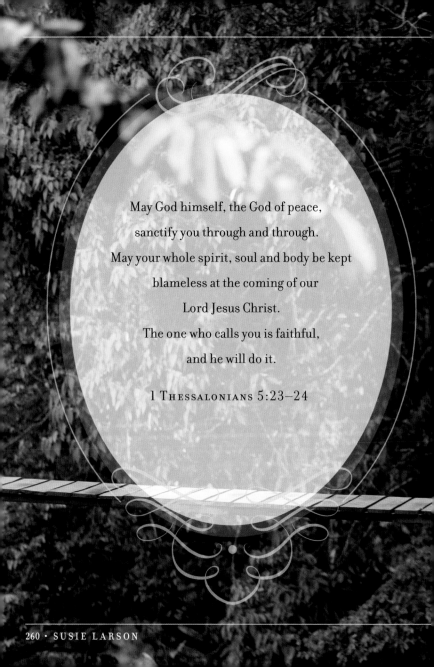

May God himself, the God of peace,

sanctify you through and through.

May your whole spirit, soul and body be kept

blameless at the coming of our

Lord Jesus Christ.

The one who calls you is faithful,

and he will do it.

1 Thessalonians 5:23–24

# In Step With Him

May you be so in tune with the Holy Spirit's movement in your life that you're always in the right place at the right time.

May your every step be ordered by the Lord.

May you go where He'd have you go, say what He'd have you say, and pray what He'd have you pray.

May you be a vessel that Jesus fills up and pours out on a dry and thirsty land.

And may your own soul be replenished in the process.

Have a great day today!

Faith is the confidence

that what we hope for will

actually happen;

it gives us assurance

about things

we cannot see.

HEBREWS 11:1 NLT

# Faith-Filled Eyes

May you choose to be grateful when you would rather be grumpy.

May you choose to rejoice in God's goodness when you are tempted to rehearse man's badness.

May you sing into your empty well, trusting that God will soon fill it.

And may you live with the expectancy that any day now, the Lord will bring the breakthrough.

Find peace tonight in the knowledge that more rests on God's shoulders than on yours. He's got you.

Good night!

Surely, Lord,
you bless the righteous;
you surround them with your
favor as with a shield.

Psalm 5:12

# Surrounded With Favor

May God surround you with His favor as with a shield.

May you walk with humble confidence knowing
that you have everything you need because you
have Him.

May your eyes of faith help you see what you
cannot see on your own.

May your sense of God's purpose keep you moving
forward.

And may He anoint you to walk through life
totally and completely transformed.

God is on your side.

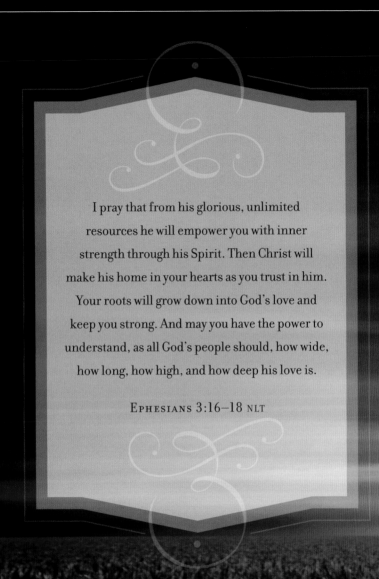

I pray that from his glorious, unlimited
resources he will empower you with inner
strength through his Spirit. Then Christ will
make his home in your hearts as you trust in him.
Your roots will grow down into God's love and
keep you strong. And may you have the power to
understand, as all God's people should, how wide,
how long, how high, and how deep his love is.

Ephesians 3:16–18 nlt

# Rooted in Love

May God himself lift you up and make you strong.

May He intervene where you cannot.

May He shine His light on the enemy's schemes.

May He confuse the enemy's plans and profoundly answer your prayers.

May He establish you in His highest and best purposes for your life.

You matter deeply to Him.

Blessed sleep be yours tonight!

Heal me, Lord, and I will be healed;

save me and I will be saved,

for you are the one I praise.

JEREMIAH 17:14

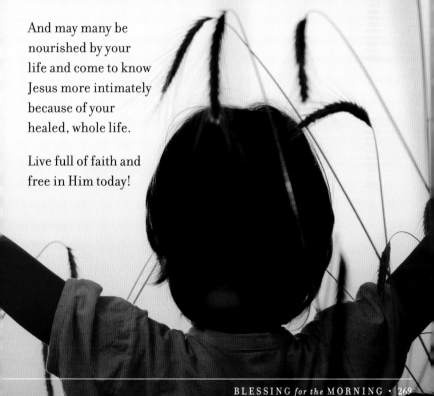

# Satisfied and Strengthened

May the Lord strengthen your frame and heal your soul.

May He satisfy your needs in a sun-scorched land.

May you receive all He so lovingly pours out on you and become like a well-watered garden, like a spring whose waters never fail.

And may many be nourished by your life and come to know Jesus more intimately because of your healed, whole life.

Live full of faith and free in Him today!

Patient endurance is what you need now,

so that you will continue

to do God's will.

Then you will receive all that

he has promised.

HEBREWS 10:36 NLT

# Reaping Results

May your hard work reap exceptional rewards.

May your earnest prayers accomplish great and powerful things.

May your faith-filled gifts produce exponential results.

And may your rest heal and restore you in every way.

Sleep well tonight.

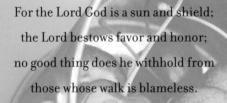

For the Lord God is a sun and shield;

the Lord bestows favor and honor;

no good thing does he withhold from

those whose walk is blameless.

PSALM 84:11

# His Goodness

May you focus more on Jesus' goodness than on your badness.

May you get excited about His supply instead of despairing over what you lack in yourself.

May you look to Him and imagine what's possible instead of looking down at what seems impossible.

God is doing a new thing in your midst.

Lean in and look for Him with expectancy today, for every good gift comes from Him and He loves His children deeply.

Choose joy this day!

Anyone who believes in me
may come and drink!
For the Scriptures declare,
"Rivers of living water will flow
from his heart."

John 7:38 NLT

# Life-Giving Water

May God bless you with spontaneous fun and hilarious laughter.

May He break through in a sudden moment with a greater-than-expected answer.

May He bless you with Sabbath moments of replenishment and rest.

And by God's grace may you impart life and healing to every conversation.

And tonight, sweet dreams.

Be strong and take heart,

all you who hope in the Lord.

Psalm 31:24

# *Be Strong, Take Heart*

May you refuse to connect the dots on your painful experiences and thus draw a wrong conclusion about yourself and God.

May you instead be hemmed in by God's powerful promises, and may you be defined by His very personal love for you.

May you refuse to let your past speak to you, except to teach you.

And may you insist on living as one who has a redemptive story to tell. You are that important to God's kingdom-story.

Walk assured today.

God is with you.

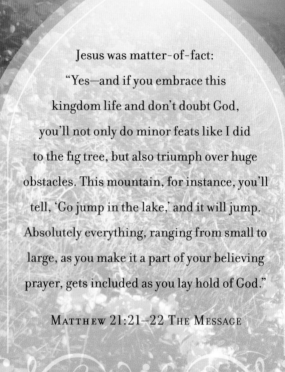

Jesus was matter-of-fact:

"Yes—and if you embrace this

kingdom life and don't doubt God,

you'll not only do minor feats like I did

to the fig tree, but also triumph over huge

obstacles. This mountain, for instance, you'll

tell, 'Go jump in the lake,' and it will jump.

Absolutely everything, ranging from small to

large, as you make it a part of your believing

prayer, gets included as you lay hold of God."

MATTHEW 21:21–22 THE MESSAGE

## Facing Down Fears

May God pour out fresh grace where life's been a grind.

May He impart peace where you've only known pain.

May He release a mighty faith to face down your fears.

And because He is faithful, may you courageously
take on the mountain in front of you.

But tonight, sleep well.

God can do anything, you know—

far more than you could ever imagine

or guess or request in your wildest dreams!

He does it not by pushing us around

but by working within us,

his Spirit deeply and gently within us.

Ephesians 3:20 The Message

# A Divinely Paced Life

May you suddenly grow in your capacity to understand God's love.

May the reality of His feelings toward you put your heart at ease and fill your soul with gladness.

May the rush and worry culture have no impact on you.

And may the Lord Himself set your pace and establish you in your purpose.

His yoke is precious, beautiful, divine, and doable.

Peace to you.

Don't be afraid,

for I am with you.

Don't be discouraged,

for I am your God.

I will strengthen you and help you.

I will hold you up with my

victorious right hand.

Isaiah 41:10 NLT

# Your Defender and Protector

May you stand strong in the face of your fears and stronger still when it comes to your faith.

May you bow low when you'd rather exalt yourself and bow lower still in the presence of God.

May you accept grace for your own missteps and offer more grace still when someone steps on you.

God is your defender and protector.

Trust in Him.

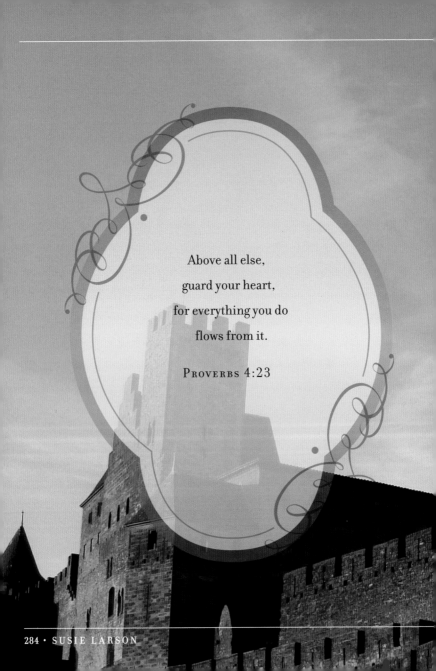

Above all else,

guard your heart,

for everything you do

flows from it.

PROVERBS 4:23

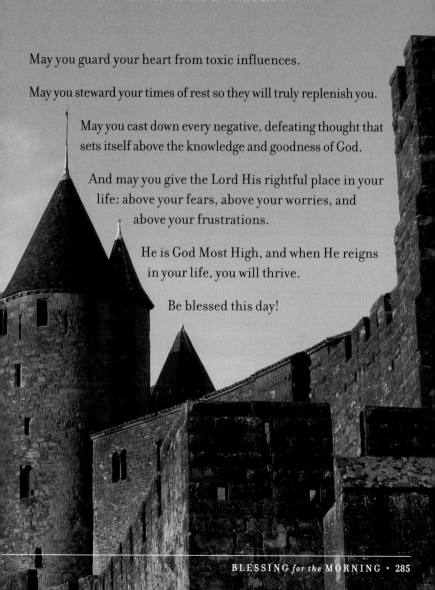

# Guard Your Heart

May you guard your heart from toxic influences.

May you steward your times of rest so they will truly replenish you.

May you cast down every negative, defeating thought that sets itself above the knowledge and goodness of God.

And may you give the Lord His rightful place in your life: above your fears, above your worries, and above your frustrations.

He is God Most High, and when He reigns in your life, you will thrive.

Be blessed this day!

How great is the goodness you have stored up
for those who fear you. You lavish it on those
who come to you for protection,
blessing them before the watching world.
You hide them in the shelter of your presence,
safe from those who conspire against them.
You shelter them in your presence,
far from accusing tongues.

PSALM 31:19–20 NLT

# Shelter in the Storm

May God draw you in so close that your heart beats
in rhythm with His.

May He keep you far from accusing tongues and critical
spirits.

May He fill your ears with words of truth, direction,
promise, and love.

May your face shine with the strong assurance
that you belong to God.

And I ask him that with both feet planted
firmly on love, you'll be able to take in
with all followers of Jesus the extravagant
dimensions of Christ's love. Reach out
and experience the breadth! Test its length!
Plumb the depths! Rise to the heights!
Live full lives, full in the fullness of God.

Ephesians 3:17–19 The Message

## *Receive, Believe, Live*

As you breathe in the morning air, may you breathe in a fresh revelation of God's love.

As you stretch your muscles and move through your day, may you also activate and stretch your faith in the promises of God.

Believe God when He says He is for you and with you.

You possess more than you need when you are in Christ Jesus.

Walk, live, and breathe like the heir of God you are.

You, LORD, hear the desire
of the afflicted;
you encourage them,
and you listen
to their cry.

PSALM 10:17

# *Glimpses of Glory*

May new breakthroughs be yours all around.

May you start to see glimpses of God's glory, tokens of your faith, and evidences that God is moving on your behalf.

May the winds start to blow, letting you know that answers to your heart's desires are on their way.

And tonight, may your sleep nourish your soul and restore your health.

Good night!

Be dressed ready for service

and keep your lamps burning.

Luke 12:35

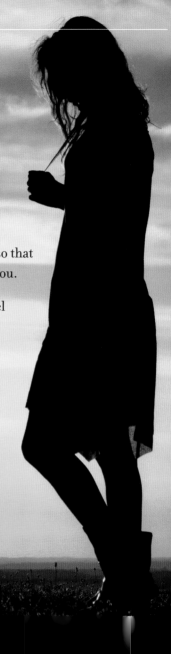

## *Ready to Respond*

May God fill you afresh with His Spirit so that you will respond in faith to the smallest nudge within you.

May you walk away from time wasters so that you may possess all God longs to give you.

May you turn a deaf ear to lies that "feel true" so you can embrace the beautiful truth that is true!

And may God's presence and love be tangible to you today.

May the God who gives endurance

and encouragement give you the same

attitude of mind toward each other

that Christ Jesus had,

so that with one mind and one voice

you may glorify the God and

Father of our Lord Jesus Christ.

ROMANS 15:5–6

## When You'd Rather . . .

May God grant you grace
when you'd rather grumble.

May He inspire hope
when you'd rather breathe a heavy sigh.

May He help you be kind
when you'd rather be cruel.

May you rest in Him tonight
and be more like Him
tomorrow.

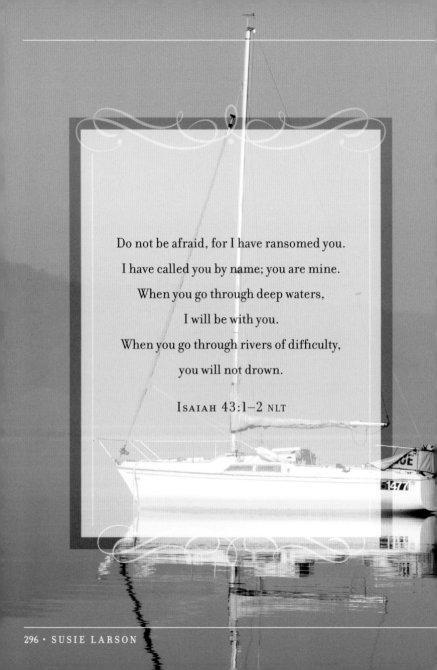

Do not be afraid, for I have ransomed you.

I have called you by name; you are mine.

When you go through deep waters,

I will be with you.

When you go through rivers of difficulty,

you will not drown.

Isaiah 43:1–2 nlt

# Do Not Fear

When you can't sense what God is up to, may you trust even more His heart toward you.

When your journey is different than you would choose, may you see His invitation to make you new.

When the storm rages overhead, may you know—with everything in you—that new mercies are on the other side.

And when you're tempted to overstate your problems and understate His promises, may you step back and find your footing again.

On Christ the solid Rock you stand, all other ground is sinking sand.

Embrace a joy-perspective this day!

I, a prisoner for serving the Lord,

beg you to lead a life worthy of your calling,

for you have been called by God.

Always be humble and gentle.

Be patient with each other, making allowance

for each other's faults because of your love.

Make every effort to keep yourselves united

in the Spirit, binding yourselves

together with peace.

Ephesians 4:1–3 nlt

# United With Christ

May God heal your broken relationships, refresh your tired relationships, and sustain your new relationships.

May He awaken in you a new awareness of His presence and His love.

And may the quality and the power of your communion with Christ transform every aspect of your life.

And tonight, may you rest well in Him.

Commit to the Lord

whatever you do,

and he will establish your plans.

PROVERBS 16:3

## God Will Move

May you throw aside your
detailed expectations
of what you want others
to do for you, and throw
your arms open with fresh
expectancy that God will
move in His time and
His way according to His
wisdom and will.

He is your source of life
and will never let you down
or forsake you.

You possess all when you have Him.

Bless your precious, faith-filled heart today!

I pray that the eyes of your heart may be enlightened in order that you may know the hope to which he has called you, the riches of his glorious inheritance in his holy people, and his incomparably great power for us who believe. That power is the same as the mighty strength he exerted when he raised Christ from the dead and seated him at his right hand in the heavenly realms, far above all rule and authority, power and dominion, and every name that is invoked, not only in the present age but also in the one to come.

EPHESIANS 1:18–21

# *Incomparable Power*

May your prayers be filled with power.

May your words be full of grace and truth.

May your God-given dreams surprise and inspire you.

And may your kindness and generosity change the world.

Sleep well. God is with you.

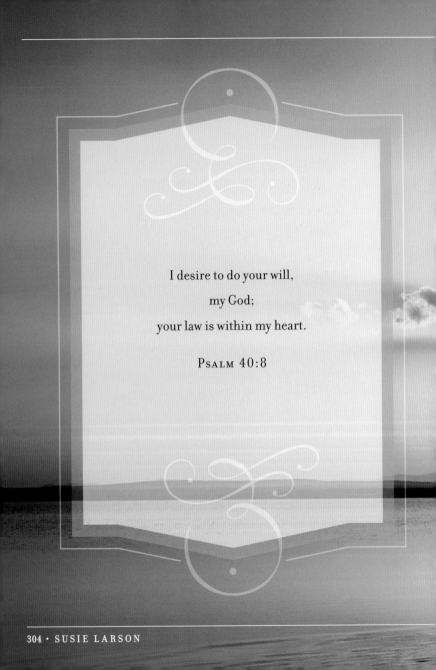

I desire to do your will,

my God;

your law is within my heart.

PSALM 40:8

## *Live in Response to Him*

May you refuse the autopilot life.

May you instead be a lean-in-and-listen kind of person.

May you be quick to discern the Lord's whisper and quick to follow His lead.

May you notice the winds of change
blowing in the trees and loosen
your tent stakes if the Lord
requires it.

And may you
cup your ear toward
heaven and treasure the Lord's voice above all others.

Enjoy your day today!

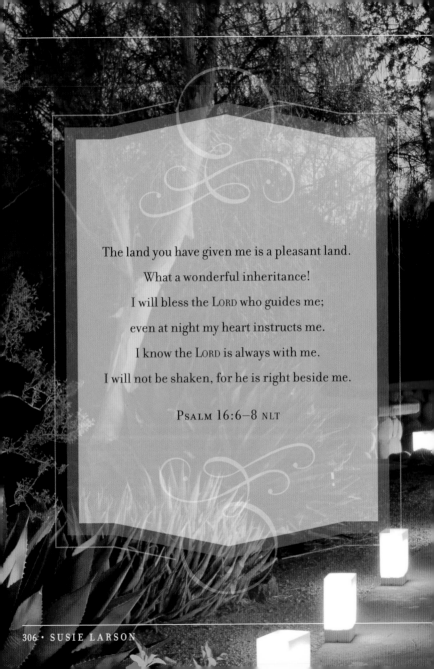

The land you have given me is a pleasant land.

What a wonderful inheritance!

I will bless the LORD who guides me;

even at night my heart instructs me.

I know the LORD is always with me.

I will not be shaken, for he is right beside me.

PSALM 16:6–8 NLT

# An Ever-Present Help

As the day wraps up and you crawl into bed tonight, may your body, mind, and soul be at rest and know the deep, abiding peace that comes from deeply knowing God.

May He speak to you while you sleep and may He download fresh insight and perspective regarding your current circumstances.

And as you rise up in the morning, may faith rise up in you and compel you to obey when you'd rather self-protect, give when you'd rather hoard, and trust when you're tempted to worry.

You're not made for this place. You're only passing through.

Live as one who is spoken for.

Good night!

Blessed are those who fear the Lord,

who find great delight in his commands.

Their children will be mighty in the land;

the generation of the upright

will be blessed.

Psalm 112:1–2

# He Loves Your Loved Ones

May you learn to rest in the goodness of God.

When you're tempted to worry about your loved ones,
may you instead rejoice that your Savior runs after them
with an earnest love, deep compassion, and profound
wisdom. He longs to be gracious to them and show them His
lovingkindness.

May you feel free to exhale your worries and breathe in His
promises because they are true and they're for you.

It's time to refuse angst and remember that He is God, He is
good, and He cares about every detail of your life.

Walk blessed today because you are!

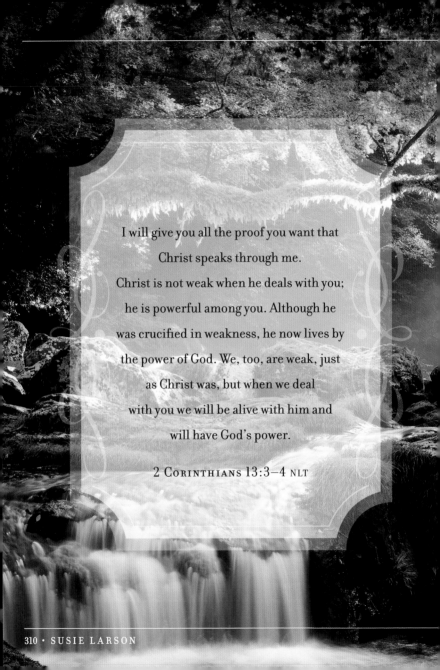

I will give you all the proof you want that
Christ speaks through me.
Christ is not weak when he deals with you;
he is powerful among you. Although he
was crucified in weakness, he now lives by
the power of God. We, too, are weak, just
as Christ was, but when we deal
with you we will be alive with him and
will have God's power.

2 Corinthians 13:3–4 NLT

# When You Are Weak

May God replace your painful
memories with redemptive dreams.

May He heal old wounds and pour in timeless wisdom.

May He shore up your weaknesses and shine through your
strengths.

And tonight, may your sleep replenish you in every way.

You are loved and blessed.

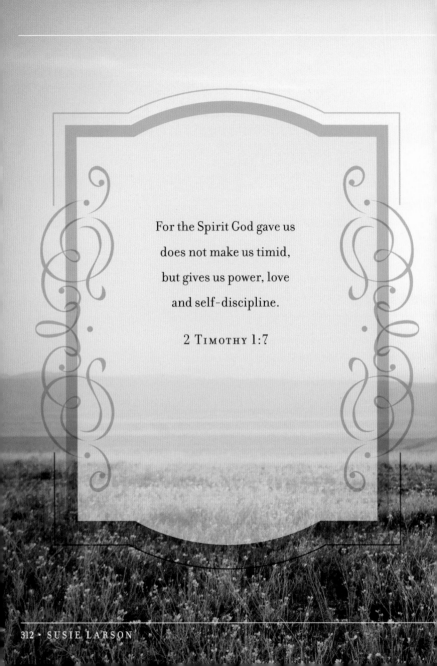

For the Spirit God gave us
does not make us timid,
but gives us power, love
and self-discipline.

2 Timothy 1:7

# *He'll Empower You*

May God Himself lift you up and encourage you today!

Where you're weary, may He revive and replenish you.

Where you're discouraged, may He infuse strength.

Where you're feeling snarky, may He calm you and make you gracious.

And where you're afraid, may He fill you with faith.

Life is hard but God is good, and He is with you every step of the way, today and every day!

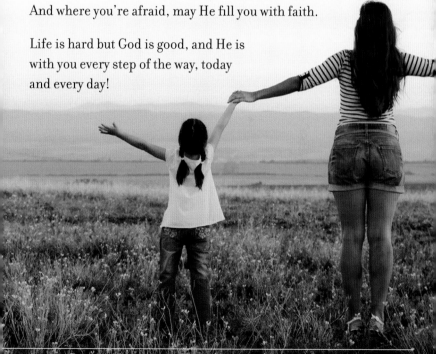

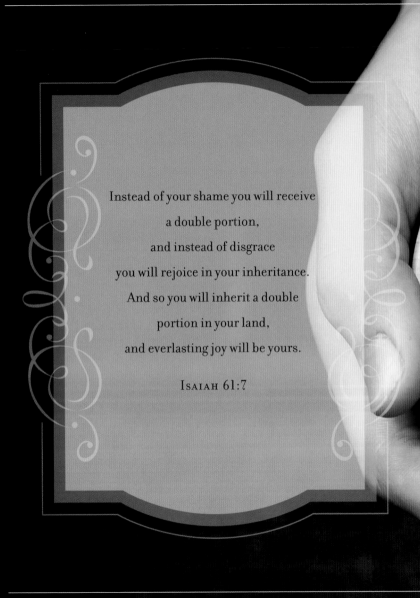

Instead of your shame you will receive

a double portion,

and instead of disgrace

you will rejoice in your inheritance.

And so you will inherit a double

portion in your land,

and everlasting joy will be yours.

Isaiah 61:7

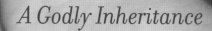

# A Godly Inheritance

May the Lord take your frustrations and give you peace; may He carry your burdens and give you grace; may He fill your cup and give you joy.

May peace, grace, and joy mark your life in a beautiful, noticeable way that compels others to look up.

And tonight may He give you divine dreams that nourish your soul and strengthen your faith.

Sleep well. You are blessed.

Nehemiah said, "Go and enjoy choice
food and sweet drinks, and send some to
those who have nothing prepared.
This day is holy to our Lord.
Do not grieve, for the joy of the Lord
is your strength."

Nehemiah 8:10

# Bursts of Joy

May God give you a burst of energy to tackle the tasks that you
need to get done.

May He inspire you to turn up the radio and dance in your
kitchen.

May He fill you with such joy that you suddenly realize just
how rich you really are.

May He connect you with an old friend and bless
you with a new friend.

And may He use you
in surprising ways
to be a blessing
to everyone you
meet today.

Have a bursting-with-
joy day today!

Take delight in the LORD,

and he will give you

the desires of

your heart.

PSALM 37:4

## Desires of Your Heart

May the Lord fulfill the desires
of your heart and stir up a fresh
passion for His Word.

May He lift a load you're not assigned to carry.

And may He strengthen you to carry your very
important God-assignment.

Sleep well.

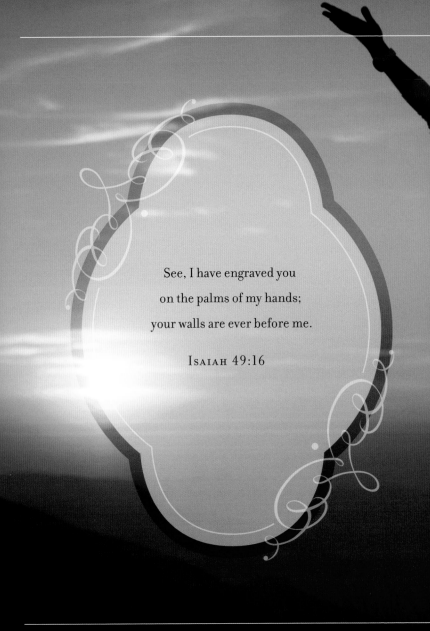

See, I have engraved you

on the palms of my hands;

your walls are ever before me.

Isaiah 49:16

## You're Someone He Loves

May you know in your core being
that you are not defined by your past
mistakes.

May you humbly understand that neither are you defined by your accumulated
achievements.

You are someone God loves.

You bear the image of the Most High God.

Your name is written on His hand; your
desires are close to His heart.

The fact that you're on the heart and
mind of almighty God is what makes you
a priceless, worthwhile treasure.

Live life according to the fullness
of that truth.

And now, dear
brothers and
sisters, one final thing.
Fix your thoughts on what
is true, and honorable, and right,
and pure, and lovely, and admirable.
Think about things that are excellent and
worthy of praise. Keep putting into practice
all you learned and received from me—
everything you heard from me and
saw me doing. Then the God of
peace will be with you.

Philippians
4:8–9 NLT

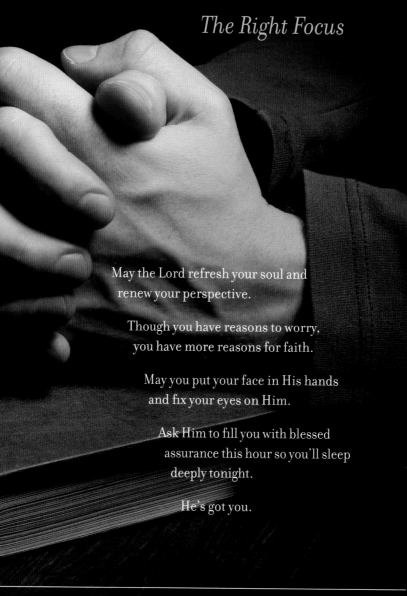

# The Right Focus

May the Lord refresh your soul and
renew your perspective.

Though you have reasons to worry,
you have more reasons for faith.

May you put your face in His hands
and fix your eyes on Him.

Ask Him to fill you with blessed
assurance this hour so you'll sleep
deeply tonight.

He's got you.

I keep asking that the God of
our Lord Jesus Christ, the glorious Father,
may give you the Spirit of wisdom
and revelation, so that you
may know him better.

Ephesians 1:17

# Know Him More

May Jesus stir up in you a fresh hunger and passion to know Him more intimately.

May He give you a gift of faith that swallows up your fears.

May He plant a dream in your soul that fits you perfectly.

And may He show you the sacred path you must take to lay hold of it.

Have a blessed and restful day!

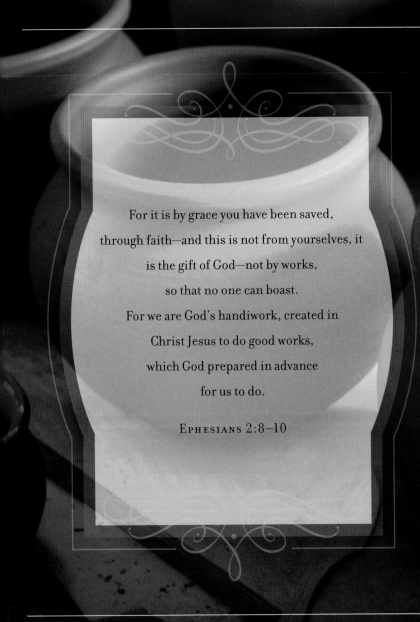

For it is by grace you have been saved,
through faith—and this is not from yourselves, it
is the gift of God—not by works,
so that no one can boast.
For we are God's handiwork, created in
Christ Jesus to do good works,
which God prepared in advance
for us to do.

EPHESIANS 2:8–10

## Created for Good

May you have eyes to see God's best will in every situation; may you have ears to hear His precious voice at every turn.

May you have words that bring hope and healing to every hardship.

And may your steps take you from one divine appointment to another.

Be safe. Sleep well.

You are loved.

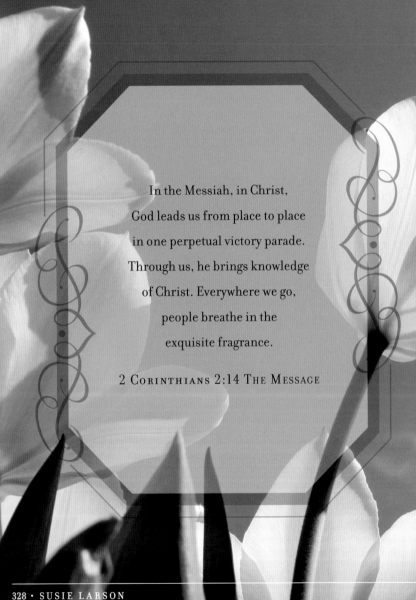

In the Messiah, in Christ,
God leads us from place to place
in one perpetual victory parade.
Through us, he brings knowledge
of Christ. Everywhere we go,
people breathe in the
exquisite fragrance.

2 Corinthians 2:14 The Message

# *Before the Breakthrough Comes*

May God give you extra grace to thrive even when your heart is breaking.

May you enjoy spilling-over-joy even before the breakthrough comes.

May you find cause to celebrate and rejoice over all that is right in your world.

Refuse to let worry have the last say.

God is the Redeemer and makes all things new.

Never give up hope.

May you dare to believe that your latter days may be more blessed than your former days.

Walk in faith today.

For the L&#x1d0d;&#1d0d;&#1d05; your God
is living among you.
He is a mighty savior.
He will take delight in you
with gladness.
With his love, he will calm
all your fears.
He will rejoice over you
with joyful songs.

Zᴇᴘʜᴀɴɪᴀʜ 3:17 ɴʟᴛ

# *Healing Joy*

May God unearth the unsettled and unhealed places
in your life so He can heal, renew, and restore you.

May He give you a new revelation of His love
and His grace.

May He give you pools of blessing to splash your feet in.

May His unfathomable greatness bring a fresh
mystery and power to your prayers and perspective.

And tonight, may you sleep deeply and sweetly.

I wait for the Lord,

my whole being waits,

and in his word

I put my hope.

PSALM 130:5

## *Any Day Now*

May you become powerful in God as you
wait for your breakthrough. In this "not yet"
season, may you learn the secret of abiding
in Him.

May you send your roots down into His
marvelous love, and instinctively trust that
He has your absolute best in mind.

May you be so acquainted with His Word and His
presence that you—right here, right now—plant
seeds of faith for a future harvest.

Instead of angst over your "not yet," may you
embrace awe for the reality of your faith, the
substance of His promises, and the surety that any
day now HE WILL BREAK THROUGH!

A single day in your courts is better than a thousand anywhere else! I would rather be a gatekeeper in the house of my God than live the good life in the homes of the wicked. For the LORD God is our sun and our shield. He gives us grace and glory. The LORD will withhold no good thing from those who do what is right. O LORD of Heaven's Armies, what joy for those who trust in you.

PSALM 84:10–12 NLT

# New Heights

May God impart to you
a new level of faith and
expectancy.

May He stir up a new passion for
serving Him.

May He release in you a new level of insight and
grant you a sharper perspective.

May He lead you to new heights with Him so you can believe
Him for great things!

And tonight, may you sleep deeply.

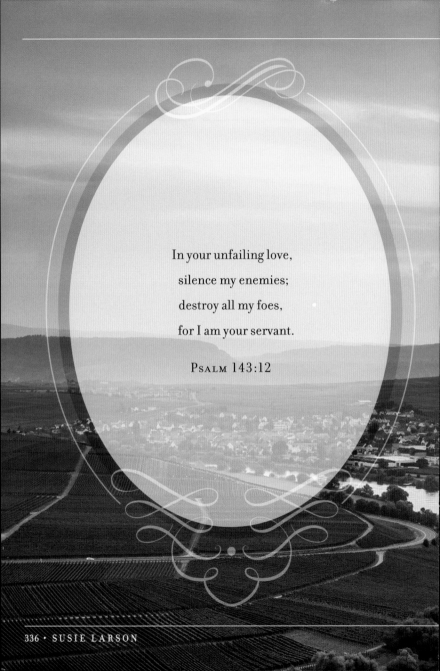

In your unfailing love,

silence my enemies;

destroy all my foes,

for I am your servant.

Psalm 143:12

# Treasures in the Valley

If you're walking through a dark valley, may you hear God's promise to you: "I will give you treasures in this valley! Riches stored in secret places!"

May you walk forward unafraid and full of faith that He'll fill your arms with spoils from this war and treasures to share with others who need what you'll learn.

Be strong and take heart.

God is near even if you can't feel Him.

He's for you, with you, and making a way where there is no way.

Don't give up. You'll be richer for the battle.

Blessings on your day today!

See, I have engraved you

on the palms of my hands;

your walls are ever before me.

ISAIAH 49:16

# In (and From) God's Hands

May you know, on a
deeper level, how much
God loves you.

May you understand in
your heart and mind
how rich you are
because of Him.

May you walk in holy confidence because
you lack no good thing.

And may you remain gracious and humble
because you know that every gift is from Him.

Sleep well.

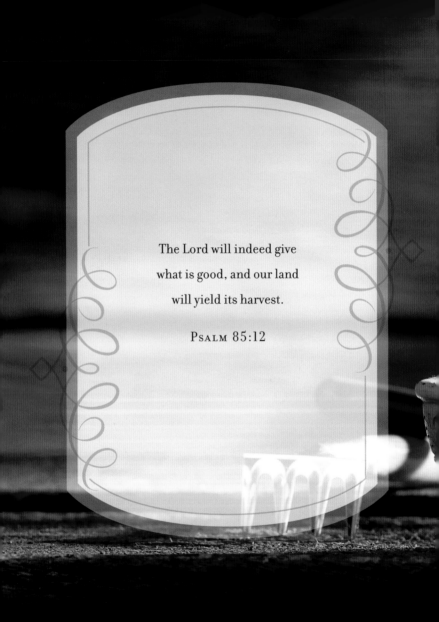

The Lord will indeed give
what is good, and our land
will yield its harvest.

Psalm 85:12

## Pray, Plant, and Believe

May you understand—on a whole new level—
how much God is for you.

May you see wonders unfold before you that
remind you how much it matters that you pray.

May you plant new seeds of faith, expectant that
you'll see a harvest in the days to come.

May you take a few faith steps today even if you
don't feel like it.

And may you invite God to heal a deep soul wound that
has plagued you for far too long.

It's a new season.

Be strong in the Lord!

May God give you more and more grace and peace as you grow in your knowledge of God and Jesus our Lord. By his divine power, God has given us everything we need for living a godly life. We have received all of this by coming to know him, the one who called us to himself by means of his marvelous glory and excellence.

2 PETER 1:2–3 NLT

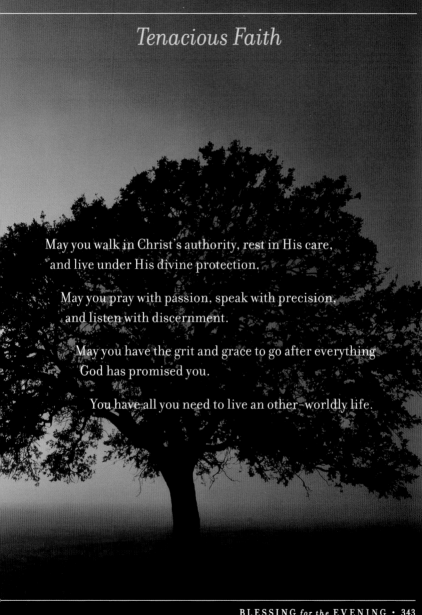

# Tenacious Faith

May you walk in Christ's authority, rest in His care,
and live under His divine protection.

May you pray with passion, speak with precision,
and listen with discernment.

May you have the grit and grace to go after everything
God has promised you.

You have all you need to live an other-worldly life.

He will yet fill your mouth with laughter
and your lips with shouts of joy.

JOB 8:21

# Surprised by Joy

May God surprise you today with oasis moments of refreshment and encouragement.

May He delight your heart with a kind and unexpected word.

May He use you to be a source of refreshment to many.

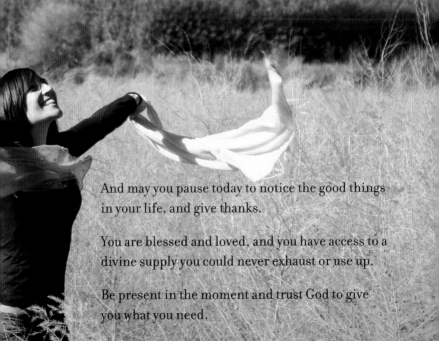

And may you pause today to notice the good things in your life, and give thanks.

You are blessed and loved, and you have access to a divine supply you could never exhaust or use up.

Be present in the moment and trust God to give you what you need.

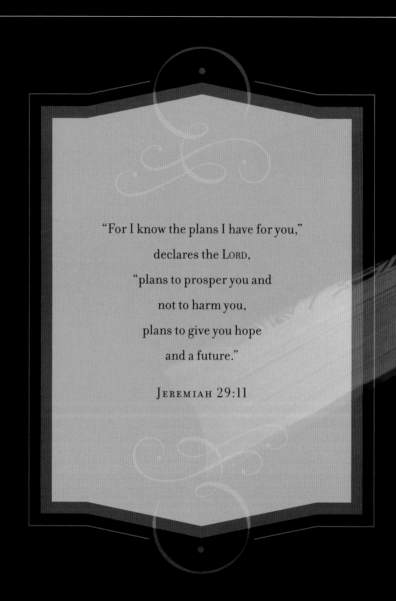

"For I know the plans I have for you,"

declares the LORD,

"plans to prosper you and

not to harm you,

plans to give you hope

and a future."

JEREMIAH 29:11

# Your Divine Purpose

May God himself pour out a fresh anointing on your passions, a fresh fire on your convictions, and the oil of joy into your soul.

May you take your first steps into tomorrow with deep insight, focused purposefulness, and Christlike love.

And tonight, may the Lord download fresh revelation about your life and your divine purpose even while you sleep.

A blessed and beautiful night to you.

Receive and experience
the amazing grace of the Master,
Jesus Christ, deep,
deep within yourselves.

PHILIPPIANS 4:23 THE MESSAGE

# *Receive!*

May you lift your head, open your arms, and receive all God so lovingly wants to pour into you today.

May you shake off the cloak of discouragement and leave it on the ground where it belongs.

God is doing a new thing in your midst!

He's already at work on your behalf.

Do not fix your mind on the things that frustrate you or break your heart.

Fix your eyes on the Author and Finisher of your faith, who will complete what He started!

Walk with faith and hope and love today!

Attention, all! See the marvels of God!
He plants flowers and trees all over the
earth, bans war from pole to pole,
breaks all the weapons across his knee.
"Step out of the traffic!
Take a long, loving look at me,
your High God, above politics,
above everything."

PSALM 46:8–10 THE MESSAGE

# Unhurried Days

May you step out of the hurriedness of the day and step into a pace that allows for face-to-face conversation with those you love.

May you tighten your belt of truth and let go of the lie that says you carry your burden alone.

May you set your face like flint and trust God's promise to carry and establish you.

And may you enjoy deep healing sleep tonight.

Your Redeemer is strong.

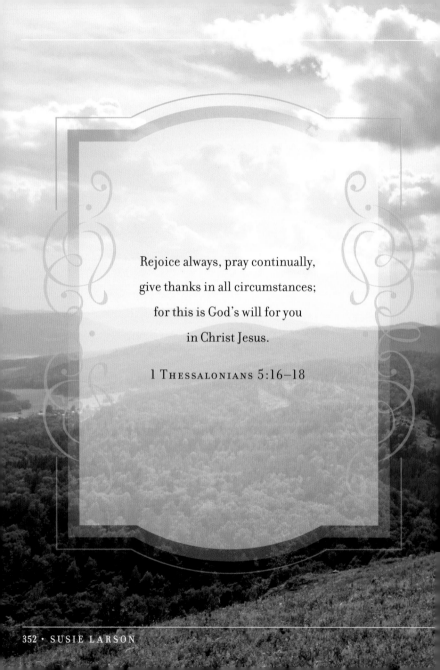

Rejoice always, pray continually,
give thanks in all circumstances;
for this is God's will for you
in Christ Jesus.

1 Thessalonians 5:16–18

# Pray Powerfully

May God revive your heart for
earnest, consistent prayer.

May you remember once again that God
moves on every act prompted by your faith.

May you rejoice in the fact that God keeps His
promises and answers prayers.

Even though you can't see it yet, Jesus has
created a stream in the desert for you. He's
made a way where there's been no way. And
soon you will see the breakthrough.

So rejoice today!

Pray today!

Believe today!

Surely the righteous will never be
shaken; they will be remembered
forever. They will have no fear of
bad news; their hearts are steadfast,
trusting in the LORD. Their hearts are
secure, they will have no fear;
in the end they will look in triumph
on their foes.

PSALM 112:6–8

# A Secure Heart

May your capacity for the things of God increase and your understanding of His love exponentially grow.

May your faith in His promises be steadfast and your view of yourself be healed because He loves you.

Sleep well.

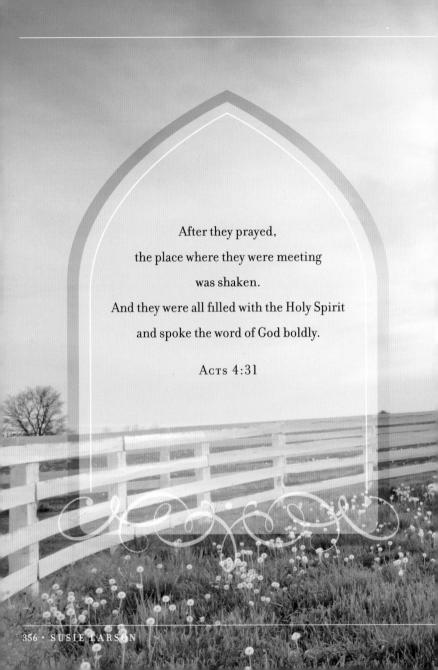

After they prayed,

the place where they were meeting

was shaken.

And they were all filled with the Holy Spirit

and spoke the word of God boldly.

ACTS 4:31

# God Is Near

May God's Spirit stir up your faith and quicken your heart
so you sense His nearness like never before.

May His power mark your life, the way you pray,
and what you say.

May His love fill you and spill out of you to the broken
and hurting souls in your midst.

As you delight deeply in Him, may He overwhelm
you with the deep desires of your heart.

Worship Him passionately today!

Because of the LORD's great love
we are not consumed,
for his compassions never fail.
They are new every morning;
great is your faithfulness.
I say to myself,
"The LORD is my portion;
therefore I will wait for him."

LAMENTATIONS 3:22–24

# Morning Mercies

May you rest tonight knowing that fresh mercies will greet you
in the morning, grace will cover you throughout the day, and
God's power will be available to you when you need it.

May regret, shame, and insecurity be far removed from you.

May holy confidence and humble dependence mark
your life in every way.

Sleep deeply tonight.

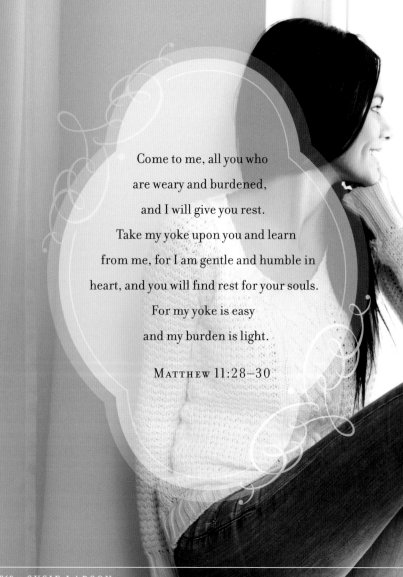

Come to me, all you who
are weary and burdened,
and I will give you rest.
Take my yoke upon you and learn
from me, for I am gentle and humble in
heart, and you will find rest for your souls.
For my yoke is easy
and my burden is light.

Matthew 11:28–30

# Rest While He Works

May the phrase "Let go and let God" take on a whole new meaning for you.

May you learn to rest while He works on your behalf.

May you understand your role in this kingdom-story and do only what He tells you to do.

May you live free from the bondage of others' opinions so you're free to love them the way Christ does.

And may others be so drawn to your healed heart that they come to know Jesus for themselves.

Rest in Him.

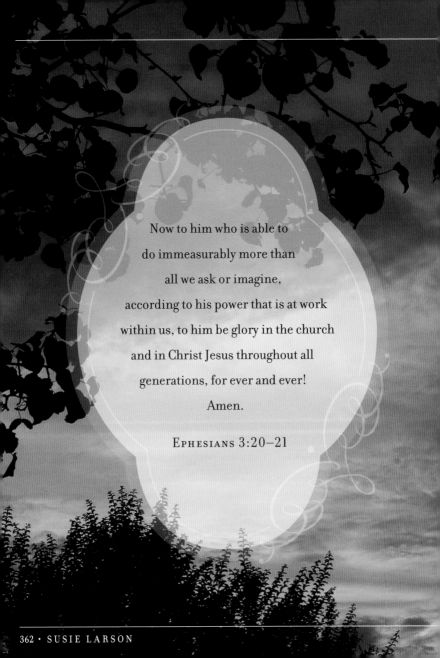

Now to him who is able to
do immeasurably more than
all we ask or imagine,
according to his power that is at work
within us, to him be glory in the church
and in Christ Jesus throughout all
generations, for ever and ever!
Amen.

EPHESIANS 3:20–21

# From Impossible to Possible

(Speak this over yourself):

I am deeply loved, divinely appointed,
abundantly equipped, and profoundly
  cherished by God.

No enemy plan, scheme, or obstacle can keep me
  from God's highest and best will for me.

As I follow the voice of my Savior, I see the invisible,
  accomplish the impossible, and love the unlovable.

I am a living, breathing miracle because
  Jesus Christ lives in me!

  Amen.

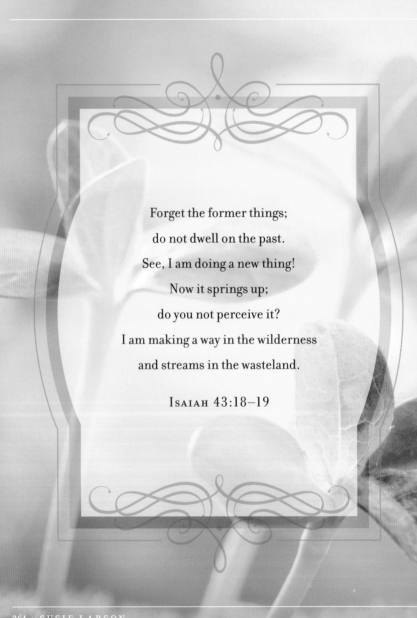

Forget the former things;

do not dwell on the past.

See, I am doing a new thing!

Now it springs up;

do you not perceive it?

I am making a way in the wilderness

and streams in the wasteland.

Isaiah 43:18–19

# Rest, Revival, and Renewal

May this next season for you be one of rest, revival, and renewal.

May you experience the REST of God in your most trying circumstances, and as a result, find peace and bear fruit where there's only been angst and thorns.

May you experience a personal REVIVAL that changes how you pray, what you say, and where you put your time.

And may you experience such soul RENEWAL that even the old things in your life feel new.

God doesn't make things "nice," He makes things new.

Trust Him to do a brand-new work in you in the days ahead.

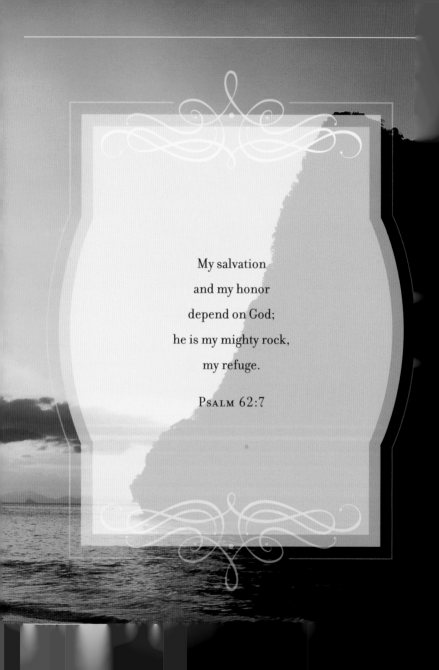

My salvation

and my honor

depend on God;

he is my mighty rock,

my refuge.

PSALM 62:7

# Release Your Burdens

As you end your day, may you release your burdens
and cling more firmly to faith.

May you release your criticisms and choose
to believe the best.

And may you rest in the knowledge that both
your salvation and your honor depend on God alone.

He is your mighty rock and refuge.

You did not choose me,

but I chose you and appointed you

so that you might go and bear fruit—

fruit that will last—and so that whatever

you ask in my name

the Father will give you.

This is my command:

Love each other.

John 15:16–17

# Divinely Called

May you begin to see your disappointments as divine appointments.

May your Spirit eyes open up to God's invitation to something better, something deeper, something profoundly fitted for you.

May you lift your eyes and see how your whole story fits in the bigger story God is writing for His Namesake.

God intends to solve some of the world's problems through you.

Trust Him and let Him use you in ways that are beyond you!

Look for those appointments, and have a great day.

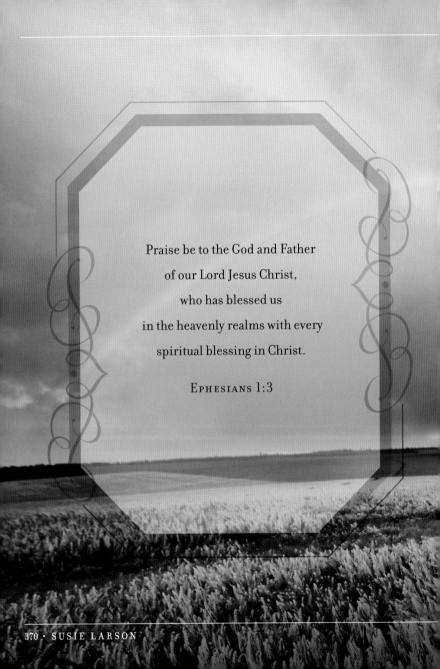

Praise be to the God and Father

of our Lord Jesus Christ,

who has blessed us

in the heavenly realms with every

spiritual blessing in Christ.

EPHESIANS 1:3

# An Unlimited Supply

May God grant you a fresh perspective of His unlimited supply.

May you trust Him
with your needs and desires.

May He breathe fresh life into your
soul and fresh power into your dreams.

May you refuse to let your fears and insecurities
speak louder than God's voice.

Even as you sleep, may your ears be fine-tuned to heaven's
song over you, for it is redemptive, beautiful, and life-giving!

Rest well.

# Blessings for Specific Needs and Occasions

A Restful Weekend

Sabbath Rest

Stepping Out in Faith

Grief

No Condemnation

Spiritual Warfare

Disappointment

Thanksgiving Day

Christmas Eve

Christmas

End of Year

Let my soul be at rest again, for

the Lord has been good to me.

Psalm 116:7 NLT

# A Restful Weekend

May you have time this weekend to pause, be still, and to dream with God.

What does He have for you in the days ahead?

May you move the clutter out of the way and make room for Jesus to change your life and establish you in His purposes for you.

May the constant flurried activity be replaced by memories of how God has come through for you and absolute clarity about the things He has for you in the future.

Always remember, He is the greatest treasure of all.

Have a blessed and beautiful weekend!

There remains, then, a Sabbath-rest

for the people of God;

for anyone who enters God's rest

also rests from their works,

just as God did from his.

Let us, therefore, make every effort

to enter that rest,

so that no one will perish

by following their example

of disobedience.

HEBREWS 4:9–11

# Sabbath Rest

For the next twenty-four hours, may God help you engage in true Sabbath rest.

May you unhitch from the daily burden, the daily yoke, and the daily concerns that are yours.

May you pause long enough to pray, be present enough to enjoy another's company, and slow down
enough to rest.

And above all, may you worship
the One who gave you the Sabbath.

Sleep well!

By faith Abraham, when called
to go to a place he would later receive
as his inheritance, obeyed and went,
even though he did not know
where he was going.

HEBREWS 11:8 NLT

# Stepping Out in Faith

May you have the holy inspiration to live up to what you already know!

As you wait on God for your marching orders, may you fully believe that He'll supply your every need.

May you become a bold, brave warrior who stands in faith, trusts wholeheartedly, and testifies to what God has done.

May your life be marked by power, authority, and mostly love.

And may the reality of Christ in you mark your life in every way, so that wherever you place your feet, God's kingdom comes to earth.

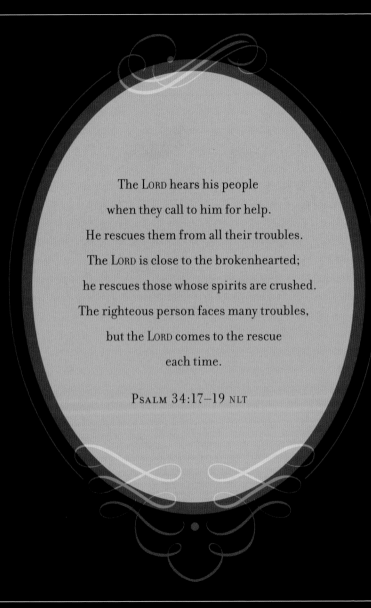

The LORD hears his people

when they call to him for help.

He rescues them from all their troubles.

The LORD is close to the brokenhearted;

he rescues those whose spirits are crushed.

The righteous person faces many troubles,

but the LORD comes to the rescue

each time.

PSALM 34:17–19 NLT

# Grief

May God himself surround you with tender mercies
and divine strength.

May He heal your broken heart and restore your sense of
hope.

May He give you precious times of rest while you work
through your grief.

And may He show you that He's not finished with you yet.

He has a beautiful plan that will bless your heart.

He'll restore and redeem every lost thing!

Rest in Him today.

Bless you.

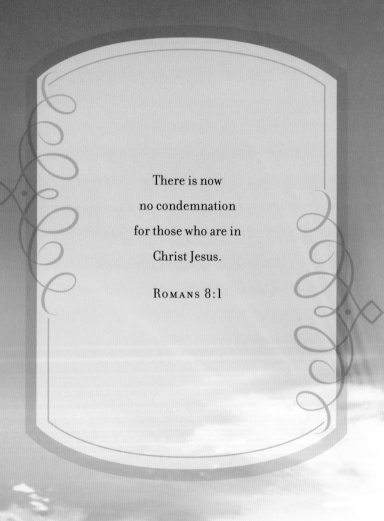

There is now
no condemnation
for those who are in
Christ Jesus.

Romans 8:1

# *No Condemnation*

May you refuse to drag your past with you another step.

May you stop right here, stomp your feet, and raise your hands in the air because Christ has set you free!

He has redeemed you, received you, and claimed you for His purposes! He has forgiven you and filled you anew with His powerful Holy Spirit.

There is NOW no condemnation for you because you are in Him and He is in you!

Walk free and full of grace—even amidst your weaknesses and frailties—because He's got you. You are one of the good gifts He offers to a world very much in need.

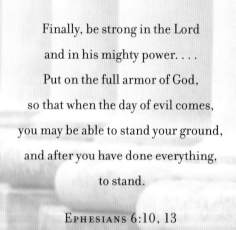

Finally, be strong in the Lord

and in his mighty power. . . .

Put on the full armor of God,

so that when the day of evil comes,

you may be able to stand your ground,

and after you have done everything,

to stand.

EPHESIANS 6:10, 13

# Spiritual Warfare

May God prove himself strong on your behalf.

May He show you how to wisely and strategically stand in this place.

May you raise your shield of faith and block every fiery arrow the enemy sends your way.

May you point your sword and dismantle every enemy scheme fashioned against you.

May you know God's loving and intimate presence right here, right now.

And may you experience firsthand how mighty, how powerful, and how faithful He truly is.

God is mighty to save, He's with you in battle, and He has equipped you to win.

May blessed and nourishing sleep be yours tonight!

Yes, I am the vine; you are the branches. Those who remain in me, and I in them, will produce much fruit. For apart from me you can do nothing. Anyone who does not remain in me is thrown away like a useless branch and withers. Such branches are gathered into a pile to be burned. But if you remain in me and my words remain in you, you may ask for anything you want, and it will be granted! When you produce much fruit, you are my true disciples. This brings great glory to my Father.

JOHN 15:5–8 NLT

# *Disappointment*

May God take all of your failures, hardships, and
heartbreaks, and carry them for you.

May you suddenly feel light in step and spirit.

May you trust that brighter days are ahead, and may you look
up expectantly as you wait for God to keep His word to you.

Rest well.

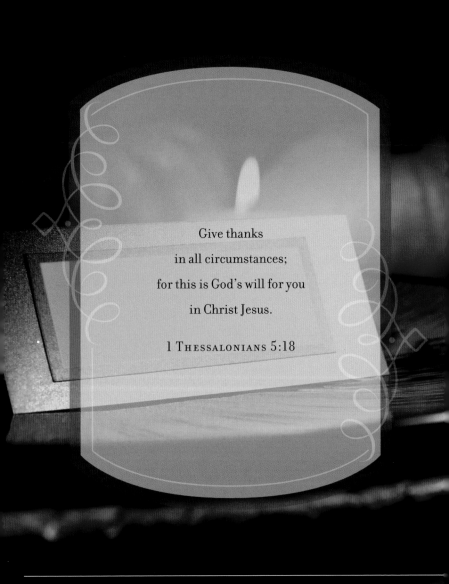

Give thanks
in all circumstances;
for this is God's will for you
in Christ Jesus.

1 Thessalonians 5:18

# Thanksgiving Day

On this Thanksgiving Day, may you set aside your fears, worries, and frustrations, and pull close the ones you love.

May you savor every bite of nourishment God provides.

May you notice sacred moments and give thanks for all that is right in your world.

May the Lord make himself especially real to you in the coming days.

And may you grow in your capacity to thank Him and trust Him.

Enjoy your holiday.

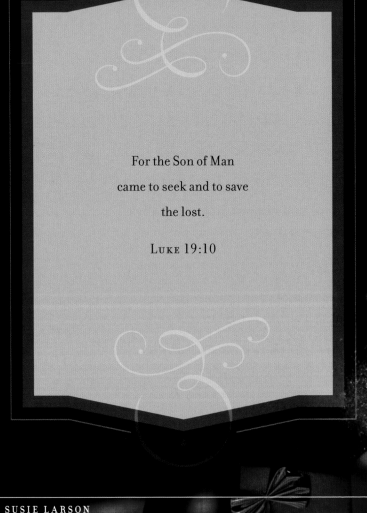

For the Son of Man

came to seek and to save

the lost.

LUKE 19:10

# *Christmas Eve*

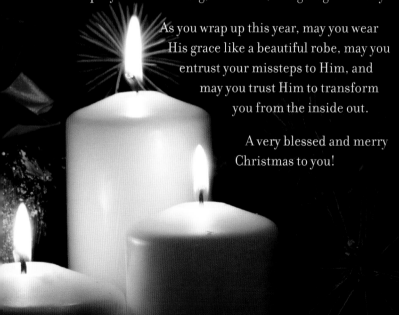

May the wonder of Christ's very personal love for you
overwhelm you and make your knees weak.

May the reality that He came to earth to seek and save the lost
give you a heart for those who've lost their way .

May the power of His Spirit within you compel you to walk by
faith and not by sight. May the promise of His unconditional
love compel you to dream big, take risks, and give generously.

As you wrap up this year, may you wear
His grace like a beautiful robe, may you
entrust your missteps to Him, and
may you trust Him to transform
you from the inside out.

A very blessed and merry
Christmas to you!

But the angel said to them,

"Do not be afraid. I bring you good news

that will cause great joy for all the people.

Today in the town of David

a Savior has been born to you;

he is the Messiah,

the Lord."

Luke 2:10–11

# *Christmas*

May you pause for a moment
today and consider this:
YOU are the object of God's
affection.

YOU are the reason Jesus came
to earth as a vulnerable baby.

YOU were the joy set before Him
when He endured the cross and scorned
its shame.

Jesus made a public spectacle of the enemy that stands against
you; He crushed the lies the enemy spews about you because
YOU are someone Jesus loves and wants forever in eternity
with Him.

Jesus IS the reason for the season.

May we joyfully celebrate the One who came as a baby and will
return as the King.

Have a most blessed, festive day today!

For I am about to do something new. See, I have already begun! Do you not see it? I will make a pathway through the wilderness. I will create rivers in the dry wasteland.

Isaiah 43:19 NLT

## End of Year

As the year wraps up and draws to a close, may you let go of any lies you picked up along the way.

May you shake off any offenses that are still hanging on. May you instead wrap yourself up in the complete love and acceptance of Christ.

May you forgive yourself and forgive others.

May you believe that God's promises are more powerful than your blunders.

May you embrace God's redemptive plan for your life with hope and expectancy.

Be healed and restored as you sleep tonight. And may you wake up with fresh faith and vision for the year ahead.

God bless you!

## Special thanks to:

*My friends at Bethany House Publishers*
*You saw the beauty in these blessings*

*My literary agent, Steve Laube*
*You gave my message wings*

*My assistant, Lisa Irwin*
*You serve in the most excellent way*

*My intercessors*
*For your consistent, faithful, powerful prayers*

*My friends and family*
*For your presence in my life*

*My Savior, Jesus*
*For all that You are to me*

**SUSIE LARSON** is a popular radio host, national speaker, and author. She hosts a daily radio talk show, *Live the Promise with Susie Larson*. Her passion is to see men and women everywhere strengthened in their faith and mobilized to live out their high calling in Jesus Christ.

Her previous books include *Your Beautiful Purpose*, *Your Sacred Yes*, *Your Powerful Prayers*, *Blessings for the Evening*, *Blessings for the Morning*, and *Blessings for Women*.

Susie and her husband, Kevin, live near Minneapolis, Minnesota, and have three adult sons, three beautiful daughters-in-law, and one adorable pit bull. For more information, visit www.susielarson.com.

May the Lord bless you
and protect you.

May the Lord smile on you
and be gracious to you.

May the Lord show you his favor
and give you his peace.

NUMBERS 6:24–26 NLT

# More Inspiration from Susie

Visit susielarson.com to learn more.

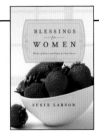

Begin each day with a reminder that God loves you with a passionate, everlasting love. Give Jesus your worries and obligations, and let Him nourish your heart, comfort your soul, and show you wisdom from His Word. Each blessing and related Scripture takes only moments to read, but is packed with a hope-filled, biblical perspective that will bring you joy and peace.

*Blessings for Women*

Respond today to that nudge in your spirit—that desire to use your gifts and passions more fully in God's work—and discover God's beautiful purpose for your life.

*Your Beautiful Purpose*

# Wisdom from Susie

Visit susielarson.com to learn more.

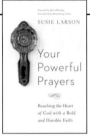

Through personal stories and biblical insights, Susie Larson shares the secrets to effective prayer in this warm and wise book. You'll be amazed at what your prayers can do when you combine reverence, expectation, and a tenacious hold on God's promises. Discover how to pray specifically and persistently with faith and joy!

*Your Powerful Prayers*

It's so easy to give away our time to things un-appointed by God. In this practical and liberating book, Susie invites you to say no to overcommitment and yes to the life of joy, passion, and significance God has for you.

*Your Sacred Yes*

⬥ BETHANYHOUSE